SHE LOOKED UP TO FIND LAFAYETTE SMILING AT HER

A LITTLE MAID

OF

OLD PHILADELPHIA

BY

ALICE TURNER CURTIS

AUTHOR OF

A LITTLE MAID OF OLD NEW YORK
A LITTLE MAID OF MARYLAND

ILLUSTRATED BY EDNA COOKE

APPLEWOOD BOOKS
BEDFORD, MASSACHUSETTS

A Little Maid of Old Philadelphia was first published by the Penn Publishing Company in 1919.

ISBN 1-55709-325-3

Thank you for purchasing an Applewood Book.
Applewood reprints America's lively classics—
books from the past that are still of interest to modern readers.
For a free copy of our current catalog, write to:
Applewood Books, Box 365, Bedford, MA 01730.

10 9 8 7 6 5 4 3 2

Printed and bound in Canada.

Library of Congress Cataloging-in-Publication Data
Curtis, Alice Turner.
    A little maid of old Philadelphia / by Alice Turner Curtis,
author of A little maid of old New York [and] A little maid of
Maryland; illustrated by Edna Cooke.
        p.   cm.
    Summary: Two girls who keep their ears open and make
good use of their knowledge play a part in the story of the
Revolutionary War in Pennsylvania in 1778.
    ISBN 1-55709-325-3
    1. Pennsylvania—History—Revolution, 1775–1783—Juvenile
fiction.   [1. Pennsylvania—History—Revolution, 1775–1783—
Fiction.   2. United States—History—Revolution, 1775–1783—
Fiction.]
I. Cooke, Edna, ill.   II. Title.
PZ7.C941Lmn   1996
[Fic]—dc20   95-49354
                                           CIP
                                            AC

Introduction

RUTH PENNELL and Winifred Merrill lived in Philadelphia. The city had been for some time in the hands of General Howe and the British army. Ruth's father was with Washington at Valley Forge, and the little girls were ardent supporters of the American cause, and admirers of the gallant young Frenchman, the Marquis de Lafayette.

Children in 1778 were much like those of today, and Ruth and her friends, eager as they were for the war to end successfully, were fond of dolls and pets, and games and little plays. Yet they kept their ears open, and when Ruth overheard what two British soldiers said she knew how to make good use of her knowledge.

In each of the other "Little Maid" books is the story of an American girl during the Revolution. The other stories are *A Little Maid of Old New York* and *A Little Maid of Maryland*.

Contents

Illustrations

A Little Maid of Old Philadelphia

CHAPTER I

HERO IS LOST

"WHERE do you suppose Hero can be, Aunt Deborah? He isn't anywhere about the house, or in the shed or the garden," and Ruth Pennell's voice sounded as if she could hardly keep back the tears as she stood in the doorway of the pleasant kitchen where Aunt Deborah was at work.

"Do you suppose the British have taken him?" she asked a little fearfully; for it was the spring of 1778, when the British troops were in Philadelphia, and Ruth was quite sure that every English soldier who saw Hero must want him for his own. The dog was her dearest possession. On her tenth birthday, nearly a year before, her father had given her Hero for a birthday present; and now that her father was with Washington's army his gift seemed even more precious to his little daughter.

Aunt Deborah looked at Ruth for a moment before she answered, and Ruth became conscious that her brown hair was rough and untidy from running about the garden in the March wind, that her hands were not clean, and that there was an ugly rent in her blue checked apron where it had caught on a nail in the shed.

"Was it not yesterday that thee declared Hero was stolen, only to find that he had followed Winifred Merrill home? And on Sunday, thee was sure he had been killed, because he did not appear the first time thee called," responded Aunt Deborah reprovingly. Aunt Deborah was not very large, and her smooth round face under the neat cap, such as Quaker women wear, was usually smiling and friendly; but it always seemed to Ruth that no least bit of dirt or untidiness ever escaped those gray eyes.

"Do you suppose he is at Winifred's? I wish she wouldn't let him follow her," and Ruth's tone was troubled. Of course Winifred was her dearest friend, but Ruth was not willing that Hero should divide his loyalty.

"Very likely," responded Aunt Deborah, "but thee must smooth thy hair, wash thy hands and change thy apron before thee goes to inquire; and put on thy hat. It is not seemly for a girl to run about the street bare-headed."

"Oh, Aunt Deborah! Only to go next door!" pleaded Ruth, but Aunt Deborah only nodded; so Ruth went to her own room and in a few minutes was back tying the broad brown ribbons of her hat under her chin as she ran through the kitchen.

"I do hope Mother will come home soon," the little girl thought as she went down the front steps to the street; "Aunt Deborah is so fussy."

Mrs. Pennell had been away for a week caring for her sister who lived in Germantown, near Philadelphia, and who was ill; and Aunt Deborah Mary Farleigh had come in from her home at Barren Hill, twelve miles distant, to stay with Ruth during Mrs. Pennell's absence.

As Ruth ran up the steps of her friend's house the front door opened, and Winifred appeared.

"Oh, Ruthie! Where are you going?" she asked smilingly.

Winifred was just a month older than Ruth, and they were very nearly the same size. They both had blue eyes; but Ruth's hair was of a darker brown than Winifred's. They had both attended the same school until Lord Cornwallis with his troops entered Philadelphia; since that time each little girl had been taught at home.

"Is Hero here?" Ruth asked, hardly noticing her friend's question.

Winifred shook her head.

"Are you *sure*, Winifred? Perhaps he ran in your garden and you didn't see him," said Ruth.

"Well, we'll see. We'll call him," Winifred replied, holding the door open for Ruth to come in.

The Merrill and Pennell houses were separated by a high brick wall, and each house stood near the street with broad gardens on each side as well as at the rear.

The two friends went through the house, and out on a narrow porch and Ruth called, "Hero! Hero!" but there was no welcoming bark, no sight of the brown shepherd dog. They went about the yard calling, and Winifred's older brother Gilbert, who was preparing a garden bed near the further wall, assured them that the dog had not been there that morning.

"Then he is lost! What shall I do!" said Ruth despairingly.

"I do believe the English have taken him. Only yesterday, on Second Street, when Aunt Deborah and I were coming home, an officer patted him and called him a 'fine dog,'" she continued quickly.

Gilbert and Winifred both looked very serious at this statement. Gilbert was fourteen years old. He was tall for his age, and thought himself quite old enough to be a soldier; but as his father and elder brother were both in Washington's army he realized that he must stay at home and take care of his mother and Winifred.

"I have a mind to go straight to High Street and tell General Howe," said Ruth, "for I heard my mother say that the English general would not permit his soldiers to take what did not belong to them."

Gilbert shook his head soberly.

"That may be true; but you are not sure that your dog has been stolen," he said. "You had best wait a while. Hero may have wandered off and may come home safely. I'd not ask any favors of America's enemies," he concluded, picking up his spade and turning back to his work.

"It wouldn't be a favor to ask for what belonged to me," Ruth answered sharply. But Gilbert's words made her more hopeful; Winifred was sure that Gilbert was right, and that Hero would come safely home.

"Come up to my room, Ruthie; Mother has given me her scrap-bag. I can have all the pieces of silk and chintz to make things for my dolls, and you can pick out something to make your Cecilia a bonnet, and perhaps a cape."

"Oh! Truly, Winifred?" responded Ruth, almost forgetting Hero in this tempting offer. The two little girls ran up the broad stairway to Winifred's room, which was at the back of the house overlooking the garden. The two windows had broad window-seats, and on one of these, in a small chair, made of stiff pasteboard and covered with a flowered chintz, sat "Josephine," Winifred's most treasured doll. Josephine wore a very full skirt of crimson silk, a cape of the same material, and on her head rested a bonnet of white silk, on the front of which was a tall white feather. There were two smaller dolls, and each occupied a chair exactly like the one in which Josephine was seated, but neither of them was so beautifully dressed.

"I made that bonnet myself," Winifred declared, as Ruth kneeled down beside the dolls and exclaimed admiringly over Josephine's fine apparel. "And that feather is one that came floating into our garden. Gilbert says it's an eagle's feather," she continued.

"It is lovely!" Ruth said, "and this window is the nicest place to play dolls in all Philadelphia. And these dolls' chairs are splendid. I wish I had one for Cecilia."

"Well, why don't you make one? I helped Grandma make these. All you have to do is cut the pieces out of cardboard, cover them with cloth, and sew them together. I'll help you," said Winifred, as she opened a closet door and drew out a brown linen bag.

"This is the scrap-bag. Look, Ruthie;" and she drew out a long strip of plaided silk.

"That would make a lovely sash for Cecilia," said Ruth, "but of course it would be nice for Josephine," she added quickly, half-afraid that she had seemed grasping of Winifred's possessions.

"Josephine doesn't like a sash," said Winifred. "You take it home and tell Cecilia it's a present from Aunt Winifred."

Then there was a roll of small pieces of pale blue satin; just right to make a bonnet for Ruth's doll.

For some time the little girls played happily with the bright pieces of silk, selecting bits for one or the other of the dolls, so that when the big clock in the hall struck twelve Ruth jumped up in surprise.

"Oh, Winnie! It's dinner-time! What will Aunt Deborah say to me?" she exclaimed, putting on her hat, and gathering up the silk pieces.

"Thank you, Winnie! I must run. Aunt Deborah doesn't like me to be late, ever," she said, hurrying toward the stairway.

"Come over to-morrow and I'll help you make a doll's chair; and I hope you'll find Hero safe at home," Winifred called after her as Ruth ran down the stairs.

At Winifred's words all Ruth's pleasure in the morning's play, in the pretty bits of silk for her dolls, and the plan for making the chairs, vanished. Hero was lost; she knew he was. With his silky coat, and his faithful, soft brown eyes, his eager bark of welcome when his little mistress came running into the garden for a game of hide-and-go-seek with him.

Aunt Deborah had spread the table for dinner, which was one of Ruth's regular duties; and when Ruth came slowly into the room she was just bringing in a dish of baked potatoes hot from the oven.

"I didn't find Hero," said Ruth, throwing her little package of silks on a chair and then her hat on top of it. "What shall I do, Aunt Deborah? What shall I do? I am sure one of those English soldiers has taken him," and now Ruth began to cry.

"Ruth! Stop thy foolish crying. Thy dinner is waiting. Go to thy room and make thyself tidy," commanded Aunt Deborah, "and take thy hat and package," she added.

Ruth obeyed rather reluctantly. "All Aunt Deborah thinks about is keeping 'tidy,'" she whispered rebelliously as she left the room. "I've washed my hands three times already to-day. She doesn't care if Hero is lost. Probably she's glad, because his paws are dirty."

But Ruth was mistaken; Aunt Deborah had spent an hour that morning in going up and down the alley looking for the missing dog, and in a careful search of the house and garden. She valued Hero's faithfulness; and not even Ruth herself would have been more pleased than Aunt Deborah to hear his bark, and see him jump forward from his usual playground in the garden.

"Perhaps Hero has wandered off," Aunt Deborah said when Ruth took her place at the table, "but he will come back, I doubt not, before nightfall."

"If he doesn't I shall go and tell the British General that he must find him," declared Ruth, somewhat to Aunt Deborah's amusement; who was quite sure that the little girl would not dare to approach General Howe, who had comfortably established himself in one of the fine houses on High Street.

CHAPTER II

Two days passed and there was no tidings of the missing dog; and even Aunt Deborah began to fear that they should never see him again. It was very difficult for Ruth to attend to the tasks that Aunt Deborah set for her; for all she could think of was Hero.

Gilbert Merrill had gone about the city making inquiries, but no one had seen Hero, or could tell him anything about Ruth's dog. Aunt Deborah was very sorry for her little niece, but she still insisted that Ruth should dust the dining-room as carefully each morning as if Hero was safe in the yard; that the little girl should knit her stint on the gray wool sock, intended for some loyal soldier, and sew for a half hour each afternoon.

Ruth dropped stitches in her knitting, for a little blur of tears hid her work from sight when she thought that perhaps her dear Hero might be hurt, unable to find his way home; or perhaps he was shut up somewhere by some cruel person who did not care if he was fed or not.

Aunt Deborah was very patient with the little girl. She picked up the dropped stitches in the knitting;

17

and when she found how uneven a seam Ruth was stitching she picked out the threads without a word of reproof.

But on the second day, as they sat at work in the little sewing-room at the top of the stairs, Ruth threw down her knitting and began to cry.

"I can't knit! I can't do anything until Hero is found. You know I can't, Aunt Deborah. And I do wish my mother would come home," she sobbed.

Aunt Deborah did not speak for a moment. She had no little girls of her own, and she often feared that she might not know what was exactly right for her little niece. So she never spoke hastily.

"For thy sake, dear child, I wish that thy mother were here: but it is very pleasant for me to have thy company, Ruth," she said in her musical, even voice. "Would thee not like to go and play with Winifred? But be sure thy hair is smooth."

But Ruth made no reply. She stopped crying, however, and looked up at Aunt Deborah.

"Didn't you like Hero?" she asked.

Aunt Deborah knitted on until she came to the last stitch on her needle, then she lay down her work, and looked at Ruth with her pleasant smile.

"Indeed, I liked Hero," she said; "but suppose I decided that because he was lost I would no longer prepare thy breakfast or dinner? that I would not see that thy mother's house was in order. Thee would truly think I had but little sense. It does not prove thy liking to cry because thy dog is lost; to fix thy thoughts on thy own feelings and leave thy tasks for me to do. It does not help bring Hero back. Now, put on thy hat and cape and we will walk toward the river. I have an errand to do," and Aunt Deborah got up and went to her own room to put on her long gray cape and the gray bonnet that she always wore on the street.

She was waiting in the front hall when Ruth came slowly down the stairs. She had put on her brown straw hat, whose ribbons tied beneath her chin, and the pretty cape of blue cloth; for there was a sharp little March wind, although the sun shone brightly. Ruth's face was very sober; there were traces of tears on her cheeks. She wished that she had said she would rather play with Winifred; but it was too late now.

"We need many things, but I fear 'twill not be easy to purchase either good cotton cloth or a package of pepper," Aunt Deborah said as they turned on to Second Street. "There was but little in the shops when the British came, and of that little they have taken for themselves so there is not much left for the people."

"They have taken Hero, I know they have!" Ruth replied. "I wish Washington would come and drive the English out."

"Oh! Ho! So here is a small rebel declaring treason right to the face of an officer of the King!" and Ruth, surprised and frightened, felt a hand on her shoulder, and looked up to find a tall soldier in a red coat with shining buttons and bands of gilt looking at her with evident amusement.

"You had best whisper such words as those, young lady," he added sternly, and passed on, leaving Ruth and Aunt Deborah standing surprised and half-frightened.

"This is an American city," Aunt Deborah announced calmly, as they walked on. "These intruders can stay but a time. But they have sharp ears, indeed. Does thee know why thy father named thy dog 'Hero'?" she continued, looking down at Ruth.

"Oh, yes! Father said 'hero' meant courage and honor; and so it was the right name for such a fine dog," Ruth answered quickly. "Aunt Deborah! What was that?" she added, stopping short. For she had heard a familiar bark.

But Aunt Deborah had heard nothing. They were passing a house where a number of soldiers were sitting on the porch smoking.

"I heard Hero bark. He is in that house," Ruth declared, and before Aunt Deborah could say a word to prevent such a rash act Ruth had run up the steps.

"Have you found a lost dog, if you please?" she asked, half-frightened, when she found herself facing two red-faced soldiers who looked at her as if she were some wild bird that had flown to the porch.

Before they could reply Aunt Deborah's hand was on Ruth's arm, and the little girl heard her aunt saying: "Thee must pardon the child. She has lost her dog, and is greatly troubled. She means no harm."

The younger of the two men stood up and bowed politely, and held his hat in his hand until Aunt Deborah had led Ruth back to the street; but neither of the men had answered her question.

"Oh, Aunt Deborah! What made you? I know Hero is in that house. I heard him bark. You spoiled it all," sobbed Ruth, as Aunt Deborah, holding her fast by the hand, hurried toward home, quite forgetting the errands she wished to do.

Aunt Deborah sighed to herself. She began to fear that Ruth was a difficult child; and that perhaps she did not know the right way to deal with little girls. But she did not reprove Ruth either for her rash act or for speaking with so little regard of Aunt Deborah's authority.

"May I go in and see Winifred?" Ruth asked when they reached home, and Aunt Deborah gave her permission.

"Oh, Winifred! I know where Hero is," Ruth declared, as the two friends went up to Winifred's room, and she hastened to tell the adventures of the walk with Aunt Deborah.

"I am going back after him, Winifred, and you must come with me," she concluded.

But Winifred said that her mother was out, and that she must not leave the house until her return. She looked at Ruth admiringly.

"I think you were brave, Ruth, to ask those soldiers. But I don't believe they would give you back Hero if you do go back. Perhaps they would make you a prisoner," she said a little fearfully; and at last Ruth reluctantly agreed not to go after the dog that day.

The little girls decided that the best way would be to go straight to General Howe and tell him that one of his soldiers had taken Hero, and was keeping him from his rightful owner.

"I'll go to-morrow. But we must not let Aunt Deborah know," said Ruth, and Winifred promised to keep the plan a secret.

Now that there seemed a hope of rescuing her dog Ruth was nearly her own happy self again. Winifred got out some squares of pasteboard and very carefully marked out patterns of the back and sides, as well as for the seat, for the dolls' chair. Then she went to find Gilbert to borrow his knife with which to cut the cardboard; and before Ruth started for home the pieces were all ready to be covered. As the two little friends sat in the pleasant window-seat Winifred said: "What do you think, Ruthie! Gilbert wants to change his name. He wants us to call him Lafayette!" and Winifred laughed, as if she thought the idea very funny.

"Why, I think that is splendid!" Ruth replied, her blue eyes shining at the thought of a "Lafayette" next door to her own home. For all the children of Philadelphia knew the story of the brave young Frenchman, hardly more than a boy himself, who had left all the comforts of his Paris home to share the danger and privations of the American soldiers. He had visited Philadelphia the previous summer, 1777, soon after his arrival in America. Gilbert had seen the handsome young officer, and ever since then he had pleaded that he might be called "Lafayette" instead of Gilbert.

"If I were a boy I should wish my name 'Lafayette,'" declared Ruth. "I wish we could do something for him, don't you, Winifred?"

"Yes; but what could two little girls do for him? Why, he is a hero, and a friend of Washington's," Winifred responded. Neither Ruth nor Winifred imagined that it would be only a few months before one of them would do a great service for the gallant young Frenchman.

CHAPTER III

RUTH VISITS GENERAL HOWE

AUNT DEBORAH was unusually quiet in her manner toward her little niece when Ruth came home with the cardboard ready to be covered. She did not ask Ruth to set the table for supper, but began to spread the cloth herself.

"I will do that, Aunt Deborah. You know I always do," Ruth said, laying down the parts for the dolls' chair, and coming toward the table.

"I will do it. Thou mayst go to thy room, Ruth; I will call thee when supper is ready," Aunt Deborah replied, without a glance at the little girl.

Ruth felt her face flush uncomfortably as she suddenly recalled the way in which she had spoken to Aunt Deborah after her aunt had led her away from the porch where the English soldiers were sitting, and where Ruth was sure Hero was hidden. She went up the stairs very slowly to her own chamber, a small room opening from the large front room where Aunt Deborah slept. She sat down near the window, feeling not only ashamed but very unhappy.

"If my mother were only here I shouldn't be sent off up-stairs. I don't like Aunt Deborah," she exclaimed, and looked up to see her aunt standing in the doorway.

For a moment the two looked at each other, and Ruth could see that Aunt Deborah was trying very hard to keep back the tears.

Then the door closed, very softly, and Ruth was again alone.

"Oh, dear," she whispered, "and I promised my mother to do everything I could to help Aunt Deborah, and now she heard me say that I don't like her," and Ruth leaned her head against the arm of the big chair in which she had curled up and began to cry, quite sure that no little girl in all Philadelphia had as much reason for unhappiness as herself.

After a little she wiped her eyes, and began to think over her misfortunes: First of all, Hero was lost. Then came all the troubles that, it seemed to Ruth, Aunt Deborah was to blame for. As she said them over to herself they appeared sufficient reasons for her dislike: "She is always fussing. Always telling me to brush my hair, or wash my hands, or not to soil my dress. And I do believe she is glad that Hero is lost, and does not wish me to find him because he brings dirt into the house."

As Ruth finished a sudden resolve came into her mind. She would not wait for the next day before going to General Howe to tell her story of Hero's disappearance, and of being sure that he had been taken by an English soldier. She would go at once. If she waited perhaps Aunt Deborah would find some way of preventing the carrying out of the plan.

"Perhaps if General Howe thought I was a grown-up lady, or nearly grown up, he would pay more attention than to what a little girl might ask," thought Ruth. And then a great idea flashed into her mind: she would pretend to be grown up.

"I'll wear Mother's best dress, and do up my hair and wear her bonnet," she decided; and opening her chamber door she ran through Aunt Deborah's room to the deep closet where her mother's best dress, a pretty gown of russet-colored silk, was hanging. Ruth pulled it down, slipped it on over her dress of stout brown gingham, and began to fasten it.

"I didn't know my mother was so big," she thought regretfully, as she managed to turn back the long sleeves, and glanced down at the full breadths of the skirt which lay in a big waving circle about her feet. "I'll have to hold it up as high as I can to walk at all."

In a few minutes the dress was fastened, and she managed to pin up her hair; and now she drew out the bandbox containing her mother's best bonnet. It was made of a pretty shade of brown velvet, with a wreath of delicate green leaves, and strings of pale green ribbon.

Ruth tied the strings firmly under her chin. The bonnet came well down over her face, nearly hiding her ears, but the little girl thought this was very fortunate, as it would prevent any one discovering who she was, if she should happen to meet any friend or acquaintance.

She began to feel hurried and a little afraid that Aunt Deborah might call her to supper before she could escape from the house. Holding up the brown silk skirt, and stepping very carefully, she made her way down the stairs, opened the front door, and with a long breath of relief, found herself standing on the front porch.

The late afternoon was already growing shadowy with the approach of twilight; and there was no one to be seen on the quiet street as Ruth, holding her skirt up in front while the sides and back trailed about her on the dirty pavement, walked hurriedly along toward High Street.

"I'll walk more like a grown-up lady when I get near the General's house," she resolved. "Won't Winifred be surprised when she knows that the English General thought I really was grown up?" and Ruth gave a little laugh of delight at the thought of her friend's astonishment, quite forgetting all the troubles that had seemed so overpowering an hour before.

As she turned into High Street she found herself facing the amused stare of two young ladies who were hurrying home from an afternoon walk.

"I suppose they were laughing because I was holding up my skirt," thought Ruth, quite unconscious of her absurd appearance, "but I'll have to, for I couldn't walk a step if I didn't," she decided.

Two English soldiers were on guard at the entrance of the fine mansion that the English General had taken from its rightful owner for his own use; and as Ruth, now half afraid to go up the steps, stood looking up at them a little fearfully, one of them noticed the queer little figure, and, quite forgetting his dignity, chuckled with amusement.

"Look, Dick! Here is a lady admiring our fine uniforms," he said, calling his companion's attention to Ruth, whose gown now trailed about her, and whose bonnet had slipped to one side.

" 'Tis a lady coming to call on the General," responded "Dick," with a wink at the first speaker.

"Did you wish to see General Howe, madam?" he continued, looking down at Ruth, while his companion chuckled with delight.

"Yes, if you please," Ruth managed to reply, beginning to feel a little afraid, and wishing that she had waited until the next day when Winifred might have come with her.

"Kindly walk up the steps, madam, and I will announce you to the General," continued the young soldier, welcoming the hope of a little amusement to break the monotony of his daily duties.

" 'TIS A LADY COMING TO CALL"

Ruth obeyed, stumbling a little as she reached the top.

"And what name shall I say?" Dick asked, bowing very low.

"Mistress Ruth Dillingham Pennell, if you please, sir," Ruth replied, gaining a little courage, and trying to stand as tall as possible, hardly sure if the young soldier was really laughing at her, or if he believed her dress to be a proof of at least twenty years of experience.

" 'Twill be good sport for the General and his friends. They are just sitting down to dinner," "Dick" whispered to the other guard, as he swung open the big door and ushered Ruth into the hall, and then led the way toward the dining-room.

"What nonsense is this, Dick? We are not rehearsing any play just now," called a gay voice; and Ruth and the young soldier were confronted by a tall officer whom Ruth instantly recognized as the same who had called her a "rebel" that very afternoon on Second Street.

She became really frightened. Suppose he should remember her, and tell General Howe what she had said about Washington driving the English from the city? It might be that, just as Winifred had said, and they would put her in prison. She wished she were safely at home with Aunt Deborah. But "Dick" was speaking to the handsome young officer.

"Ah, now, Major André, 'twill be as good as any comedy you have seen in South Street," he declared, "and the General will be well pleased. No harm shall come to the child."

"Well, I'll not interfere. This is a dull town at best," responded the young officer laughingly, and without another glance at Ruth, he entered the dining-room, with a word to the soldier who stood at the door. The big door was now swung wide open by two servants in the livery of the English General. Just beyond them stood Major André, who bowed very low as Ruth entered, and said:

"General Howe, a lady who greatly desires to ask a favor of you," and Ruth found herself on the threshold of the beautiful room whose paneled walls were brilliantly lighted by many wax candles in silver sconces. The table was handsomely spread with fine china, glass and silver; and about it were seated a number of English officers.

"More comedy, André!" called a pleasant voice; "kindly bring the lady this way," and General Howe rose from his seat at the head of the table, and instantly all his guests were on their feet.

Major André held out his hand to Ruth. She well knew that this was the proper moment to make her best curtsy, and in spite of the clumsy skirt, the bonnet which kept nodding over her face, and the long sleeves that had slipped down over her hands, she managed to make a not ungraceful curtsy.

There was a little murmur of applause, and Major André smiled kindly upon her, and taking her hand led her toward the head of the table with as much grace and courtesy as if he were handing Miss Peggy Shippen herself, one of the beauties of the town, to a seat at General Howe's dinner table.

"You are a most welcome guest," declared the English General smilingly, as Ruth stood before him. "I understand you have a favor to ask of me. Whatever it is you may be very sure I will be most happy to grant it," and he smiled down at the queer little figure, quite sure that his young officer Major André had planned the whole affair for his amusement.

"If you please, sir, I want my dog," said Ruth falteringly.

CHAPTER IV

AUNT DEBORAH IS SURPRISED

YEARS after, when Ruth was really "grown up,"
she often recalled the wonderful night when she sat
at General Howe's dinner-table. For Major André
had lifted her to a seat beside the General; with a
friendly word he untied the bonnet-strings and put
the bonnet on a side table; and Ruth began to think
that it was all a dream from which she would soon
awaken to find herself safely at home. She wondered
if it really were Ruth Pennell who was answering the
General's questions about the missing Hero.

"I can do no less than try to find your dog, little
maid," he said, "for when my own dog wandered
away to General Washington's camp, in the
Germantown fray, the General sent him back to me
under the protection of a flag of truce; so, as you tell
me your father is with Washington, I must see to it
that Hero is found. That is, if one of my soldiers has
so far forgotten orders as to have taken him," for the
English General took every care that his soldiers
should do no harm to the residents of the city.

Ruth was sure that she knew the very house where
she had heard Hero's bark; and now that General

Howe had promised that a search should be made she was eager to go home, and slid out of the chair just as a servant set a plate before her.

"I must go home. I—I—ran away," she said a little falteringly, looking up at the tall General. "Will you please find Hero the first thing to-morrow?"

"Here, André! the young lady wishes to return home," said the General, "and see to it that you take her there safely, and that you find the lost Hero. And find a better plot for your next comedy," the General added, as the young officer came forward.

Ruth wondered what "comedy" meant. She did not know that Major André, whose gay good humor and charming manner made him a favorite with all, was depended upon to furnish amusement for his brother officers; or that they had at first believed that Ruth, stumbling into the dining-room dressed as a woman, was the first act of some amusing play of André's contriving. Now that it proved she was only a runaway little girl looking for a lost dog they found it amusing that the young officer should have the trouble of taking her home.

Ruth could never quite remember the manner in which the General bade her good-bye, or if she made her curtsy, or even thanked him for promising that Hero should be found.

Major André tied on her bonnet, and opening a door that led to a side entrance, led her to the street.

"Now tell me the way, and I'll have you home in a jiffy," he said pleasantly.

But it was no easy matter for Ruth to walk as rapidly as her companion; she stumbled over the skirt; the strings of her bonnet had slipped so that it kept bobbing over her eyes and had to be pushed back; and she was now so frightened at the thought of what Aunt Deborah would say that she hardly knew in what direction they were going until the young officer stopped at her own door and lifted the knocker whose rap was sure to bring Aunt Deborah hastening to answer it.

"You will not forget about Hero?" Ruth said as they stood on the steps.

"Indeed, I shall not. Be very sure I will do my best to find your dog. I will go to the house on Second Street early to-morrow," responded André, and the door swung open and Aunt Deborah, holding a candle in one hand, stood looking at them.

"Here is your little girl, madam; she has done no harm, I assure you. She did but make a friendly call on General Howe, who sent me to bring her safely home," said the young officer, hat in hand, and making his best bow.

"I thank thee for bringing the child home, sir," responded Aunt Deborah, drawing Ruth firmly over the threshold and closing the door before Major André could say another word. The young officer hurried back to the General's dinner-table, a little vexed that he bad made so much needless trouble for himself by introducing the queer little girl to General Howe.

"Slip off thy mother's dress at once, before you do it further harm," said Aunt Deborah; and Ruth, not daring to look up, hastened to obey, as she stood in the dimly-lit hall.

"I—I—only went to look for Hero," Ruth tried to explain, after a moment's silence.

"So thee had to put on thy mother's very best gown; one that she does not wear herself save on great occasions," responded Aunt Deborah, taking up the silk dress out of which Ruth had just stepped. "It is probably ruined. Go straight to bed. Thou art a wilful and unruly child," she continued, as Ruth started toward the stairway.

Aunt Deborah followed her, the dress over her arm, but she said no more until they reached Ruth's chamber.

"I believed thee safe in thy room. When thee did not come to supper I thought thee ashamed and sorry, because of the manner in which thou spoke to me; so I did not open the door. But no; thee was playing at being some one beside thy rightful self; and going to the house of an enemy against whom thy father is fighting. I know not what to say to thee, Ruth, nor how to make thee realize that thee has brought shame upon us," said Aunt Deborah.

Ruth was crying bitterly, and could make no response. Aunt Deborah took the candle and left the room, leaving Ruth to find her way into bed in the dark. She wished with all her heart that she had not worn her mother's silk gown and pretty bonnet. If they really were ruined she knew it would be a long time before her mother could replace them; for there was no extra money in the little household while America was fighting for her rightful liberties.

"None of them, not even General Howe, believed that I was really grown up. They were just laughing at me," she thought. "It would have been just as well if I had waited, and had asked Aunt Deborah if I might not go. Oh, dear! And now I have spoiled Mother's dress."

Ruth was so unhappy that she had quite forgotten that Hero might soon be restored to her.

CHAPTER V

RUTH DECIDES

RUTH slept late the next morning, and when she first awoke it was with the puzzled feeling of waking from a bad dream. Then slowly she remembered the happenings of the previous day.

The spring sunlight filled the room. From a hawthorn tree just below her window she could hear a robin singing as if there were nothing but sunshine and delight in all the world. And then the big clock in the hallway began to strike. "One! two! three! four! five! six! seven! eight! *Nine!*" counted the little girl, and with the last stroke she was out of bed.

Before she was dressed Aunt Deborah opened the door.

"Good-morning, Ruth," she said pleasantly, quite as if nothing had happened on the previous day, and that Ruth had not slept two hours later than usual. "I have brought thee thy breakfast; and thee may stay in thy room until I call thee," and Aunt Deborah set a small tray on the light stand near the window, and before Ruth could make any response she had left the room.

Ruth was very hungry. She had no supper on the previous night, and she now looked eagerly toward the little tray, which held only a bowl and pitcher. The bowl was nearly full of porridge, and the pitcher of creamy milk.

That was all very well; and she ate it all, to the last spoonful. But usually there were hot corn muffins and a bit of bacon or an egg to follow the porridge, and Ruth was still hungry.

"Perhaps Aunt Deborah forgot," thought Ruth, "but I don't believe she did. Perhaps she is only provoked at me for being late for breakfast!"

Ruth shook up her pillows, turned back the blankets of her bed, and then went to the window and leaned out. There were two robins now on the top branch of the hawthorn, and for a moment she watched them, wondering if they were planning to build a nest there.

The window overlooked the Merrills' garden; and in a few minutes Ruth saw Gilbert coming along the path toward the wall.

"Lafayette! La-fay-ette!" she called.

Gilbert looked about as if puzzled, and Ruth called again. "I'm up-stairs. Gil-bert!" and at this the boy turned and looked up, and waved his hat in response.

"I've found Hero," she called. "Honest! And an English officer is going to bring him home this very morning."

"Come on over and tell Winifred," responded Gilbert. "She has something to tell you, too. Something fine."

"I can't come over this morning. I——" but before Ruth could say another word she felt a firm hand on her shoulder, and she was drawn into the room and the window closed, and Aunt Deborah was looking at her reprovingly.

"Ruth, why did thee think I wanted thee to stay up-stairs this morning?" she asked.

Ruth shook her head sullenly. She said to herself that no matter what Aunt Deborah might say she would not answer.

"Well, my child, then I must tell thee. I hoped thee would think over thy wilfulness of yesterday; that thee would realize that thy conduct was such as would grieve and shame thy father and mother. Dost thou think it a small thing nearly to ruin thy mother's best gown? To go dressed as if in a play to the house of an enemy of thy country to ask a favor? And before that thee quite forgot thy good manners in rushing up the steps of that house on Second Street, and then speaking rudely to me, who have no wish but to be kind to thee and help thee be a good girl."

While Aunt Deborah was speaking Ruth looked up at her, a little frightened and sullen at first; then as she saw that Aunt Deborah's face was pale, that she looked as if she had been crying and was nearly ready to cry again, the little girl's heart softened, and she ran toward her aunt, saying:

"Oh, Aunt Deborah! I am sorry I spoke rudely to you. And when I said I did not like you it was only because I was cross and so unhappy about Hero. I do like you, truly I do. And, oh! I did not think about General Howe being our enemy; or that I would spoil Mother's pretty gown. I only thought about Hero." And now Ruth was sobbing, and Aunt Deborah's arm was about her.

But for a moment Aunt Deborah made no response; then she said:

"Dear child, thee has given me happiness again. And now let us both do our best until thy mother returns. But thee knows that it is right for thee to decide if thee should not be punished in some way, so that in future thee will remember not to lose thy temper, to remember thy manners; and above all not to stoop to deceit to gain thy wishes."

Aunt Deborah smiled happily at her little niece as she finished, as if quite sure that Ruth would welcome her suggestion.

Ruth smiled in response. She began to think it would be rather fine to decide on her own punishment, and resolved it should be even more severe than any Aunt Deborah would inflict.

Yes, Aunt Deborah, I will stay up-stairs all day. And I will eat only porridge for my dinner and sup-

per. I will not call from the window, and I will knit;
and not even play with Cecilia," she said eagerly.

"Very well, dear child. But beside these things thee
must say over to thyself the reason for thy punishment. Say to thyself: 'Not again will I be rude or
unkind, not again will I be thoughtless of my behav-
ior,'" said Aunt Deborah approvingly.

There was a loud knock at the front door, and
Aunt Deborah hurried away to answer it. In a moment
Ruth heard a joyous bark.

"It's Hero! It's Hero!" she exclaimed, running
toward the door. But with her hand on the latch she
stopped suddenly. She had promised that she would
not leave the room that day. She had set her own
punishment for rudeness, and for the thoughtlessness that had perhaps ruined her mother's dress.

"Oh! I wish I hadn't dressed up," she thought, as
she turned slowly away from the door, thinking of
Hero looking wistfully about for his little mistress.
She knew that Aunt Deborah would be kind to him,
but not to see Hero after he had been missing so long
was a real punishment for the little girl, and she
went back to the window and stood looking out
wishing that for a punishment she had thought of
something beside staying in her room all day.

As she looked out she saw that Gilbert was still in his
garden, that Winifred was beside him, and that they
were both making motions for her to open the window.

She shook her head soberly. She could see that Winifred was greatly excited about something, and was talking eagerly to her brother. They both looked up at Ruth's window and again motioned with waving arms for her to open it. After a few moments they seemed to realize that she had, for some reason they could not imagine, been forbidden to; and with a good-bye signal they both turned and ran toward the house.

"I do wonder what they wanted to tell me," thought Ruth. "Oh, dear! It is dreadful to stay up here when Hero is home, and when Winifred and Gilbert have a secret." She began to realize that she had set herself no light punishment.

"But it wouldn't be a punishment if I were enjoying it," she finally decided, and getting the half-finished sock from her knitting bag, she drew a small rocking-chair to the center of the room, seated herself and began resolutely to knit.

Now and then she could hear sounds from the rooms below; and once Ruth dropped her knitting and started toward the door, for she had heard Hero's plaintive whine as he waited for admittance. Then had come Aunt Deborah's voice calling him away sternly; and Ruth picked up her knitting, resolved to keep exactly to her promise. She wondered if Major André had sent Hero home in charge of "Dick," the smiling young soldier who had spoken to her on General Howe's door-steps. But most of all her thoughts centered about Winifred and Gilbert.

She heard the clock strike eleven, and realized that she was very hungry; and that an hour was a long time to wait before Aunt Deborah would bring her bowl of porridge. A shadow darkened the window, and she looked up with startled eyes to see Winifred's face pressed against the glass.

Ruth ran to the window. "How did you get up here?" she questioned in wonder.

"Open the window, quick!" Winifred responded in an anxious whisper. "The ladder wiggles about, and somebody may see me."

Ruth opened the window and Winifred crawled in, and suddenly the ladder disappeared.

"It's Gilbert. He promised to take it down as soon as I got in. What is the matter, Ruth? Has Aunt Deborah made you stay up-stairs? Did you know Hero was home? A soldier brought him." While Winifred talked she looked at Ruth anxiously, as if to make sure that nothing had really befallen her friend.

Ruth was smiling with delight at her unexpected visitor.

"Oh, Winifred! You were splendid to come up the ladder. I'm staying up-stairs to punish myself. I was rude to Aunt Deborah; and last night I dressed up in my mother's best dress and went to see General Howe!" Ruth answered.

Winifred was too surprised to reply, and Ruth went on telling of her sudden decision, and of the adventures that followed, and concluded with: "And of course I ought not to have dressed up, and I ought not to have run away. So now I am staying up-stairs all day, and all I am to have to eat is porridge and milk. I decided it myself," she concluded, not a little pleased at the thought.

"Why, Ruth Pennell!" exclaimed Winifred admiringly. "I don't know which is the most wonderful, your going to see General Howe, or your deciding to punish yourself. Begin at the time you reached the General's house and tell me everything up to now."

Ruth was quite ready to do this, and the two little friends seated themselves on the window-seat, Winifred listening admiringly while Ruth told over the story of the previous night. She had forgotten all about punishment; but a noise in the hallway and the sound of the clock striking the hour of noon made her stop suddenly in her whispered recital. "It's Aunt Deborah! Winifred, hide, quick. Under the bed," she said, at the same moment giving Winifred a little push.

Aunt Deborah came in smiling and unsuspicious, with a well-filled bowl of porridge and a generous pitcher of milk on the tray. It had been a happy morning for Aunt Deborah. Hero was safe at home, none the worse for his adventures; and, best of all,

Ruth of her own accord had declared herself to blame, and decided that her faults should be punished. It seemed to Aunt Deborah that after this she and her little niece would have no more misunderstandings. She thought it a fine thing that Ruth wished to stay by herself all that sunny spring day; and she was sure it was no light punishment.

CHAPTER VI

A DIFFICULT DAY

AUNT DEBORAH did not linger to talk with her little niece, for it was a part of her belief that idle talk was unwise. The door had hardly closed behind her when Winifred's head appeared from under the chintz valance of the bed, and she looked cautiously about.

"Has she gone?" she asked in a cautious whisper.

Ruth nodded, and Winifred now crawled out from her hiding-place.

"I'm glad she didn't see me, Ruth. For when I came to the door this morning she said you could not see any one to-day; so I thought you were being punished, and I was bound to see you. Oh, Ruth! are you to have nothing but porridge?" and Winifred looked at Ruth's tray as if she thought such a dinner would be punishment enough for a much greater offense.

"I chose it! I said I would eat only porridge," responded Ruth, beginning to think that perhaps she had been more severe with herself than had been really necessary; and she wondered, with a little regretful sigh, if Aunt Deborah was having stewed oysters for dinner; for Ruth was sure that nothing could taste better than oysters.

"I had to see you, Ruth; and it was Gilbert who thought of the ladder. He has written a play, and you are to take part in it, and so am I," continued Winifred, who had nearly forgotten her own important news in listening to Ruth's surprising story.

"'A play'?" echoed Ruth questioningly, hardly understanding her friend's meaning.

"Yes! Yes! Don't you know that the English soldiers give plays in the Southwark Theater? They dress up and make believe, just as you did last night," Winifred explained, "and Gilbert's play is like that."

"Then I don't want to," Ruth declared. "It's horrid pretending to be somebody besides yourself."

"Oh, Ruth! This isn't like what you did. It's all about Washington and Lafayette," Winifred explained eagerly, "and our pony is to be in it, and so is Hero. It's splendid; truly it is, Ruth; and Gilbert wants you to come and rehearse this afternoon, in our stable. If you are punishing yourself you can come if you wish to."

Ruth shook her head.

"No, I can't. Don't you see I can't, Winifred? I promised just as much as if somebody else had made me. I'll have to stay in this room all day, because I told Aunt Deborah that I would."

Winifred jumped up quickly. "Then I must go right home, for Gilbert said that if you couldn't take part we'd try and get Betty Hastings. She's older and taller than you, anyway, so she'd look more like Lafayette," she said, moving toward the door.

Betty Hastings lived just around the corner on Chestnut Street. She was twelve years old. She was tall for her age, and her hair was brown and very curly. She did not often play with the younger girls.

"Lafayette? Was I to be Lafayette in the play?" asked Ruth. "Oh, Winifred! Ask Gilbert to wait. I'll come over first thing to-morrow morning. You tell him I *have* to stay up here to-day. Don't ask Betty!" she pleaded, and Winifred finally agreed to try and persuade her brother to wait until the following morning before asking Betty.

"You see, it's to be a birthday surprise for Mother; and her birthday is a week from today, so there isn't much time," Winifred explained, as she started toward the door.

"Winifred! Where are you going?" Ruth whispered in alarm; and Winifred laughed at her friend's surprise to see her about to walk boldly from the room.

"I can go down-stairs so your aunt won't know it, and open the front door just as easy, and walk right out. She is in the kitchen and won't hear me," Winifred answered; and with a warning word to be sure and be at the stable at nine o'clock the next morning, the little girl opened the door cautiously and disappeared.

After Winifred had gone Ruth ate her porridge. She began to think of Gilbert's play, and of the fun it would be to take the part of the brave young Frenchman. She walked about the room, looked at Cecilia and the half-finished chair, and sighed deeply at the thought that she might be rehearsing with Winifred and Gilbert, the pony and Hero, instead of staying alone in her room.

At last she remembered her knitting, and took it up rather reluctantly. "I do wish I hadn't worn Mother's dress," she thought. And she was conscious of a little uncomfortable feeling as to Winifred's visit after Aunt Deborah's refusal to admit her.

"But I didn't ask her to come, or help her," she finally decided; although she began to wish that her friend had waited to tell her the great news until the next day and so avoided deceiving Aunt Deborah.

But at last the long afternoon ended; and when the clock struck six there was a joyous bark just outside Ruth's door, and Aunt Deborah opened it for Hero to come bounding in. He had so much to tell his little mistress, with barks and jumps, and faithful pleading eyes, that it was some little time before Aunt Deborah found a chance to speak.

"Thee had best come down to the dining-room and have supper with me. There are creamed oysters and toast and a bit of jelly. I think thee does not need porridge for another meal to-day," she said smilingly.

"I know I'll remember about Mother's dress. It has been hard to stay up here all day," Ruth answered, glad indeed that her time of punishment was over.

"But Aunt Deborah doesn't know just how hard it was," she thought as she followed her aunt down the stairs, with Hero close beside her, thinking over Winifred's great news.

As she took her usual place at the table she was glad that she had not taken Winifred's suggestion to shorten her hours of solitude. The steaming oysters sent out an appetizing odor, the toast was crisp and golden, and the tumbler of amber-colored jelly seemed to reflect the light of the candles in their tall brass candlesticks which stood at each end of the table.

"I have good news for thee, Ruth," said Aunt Deborah, smiling at her across the table. "I have word that thy mother will return early the coming week."

Ruth gave an exclamation of delight.

"Oh, Aunt Deborah! What a lot of nice things happen all together," she said. "You won't go back to Barren Hill when she comes, will you?" For Ruth began to realize that, even with her dear mother safe at home once more, she would miss the kind aunt who had been so unfailingly patient.

It was evident that Aunt Deborah was greatly pleased. Her brown eyes shone, and Ruth suddenly discovered the amazing fact that there was a dimple in Aunt Deborah's right cheek.

" 'Tis indeed pleasant that thou should wish me to stay; but I fear my house at Barren Hill needs its mistress. To-morrow is the first of April, and I must see about planting my garden as soon as possible. Perhaps thy mother will let thee come for a visit before long," she responded. "That is, if the English General will take such a great risk as to give a small maid permission to leave the city," for no one could leave Philadelphia at that time without a written permission from an English officer.

Ruth was quite sure that she should like to visit Barren Hill. She knew it was half-way to Valley Forge, where the American soldiers had passed a dreary winter, suffering from cold and hunger, while their enemies had enjoyed the comforts of American homes in Philadelphia. But now that spring had come the American people were more hopeful; they were sure their army would soon drive the enemy from the city. The people of little settlements like Barren Hill managed to carry food and clothing to the American soldiers. Aunt Deborah, just before coming to Philadelphia, had carried a treasured store of honey to Washington's headquarters, as well as clothing and food for Ruth's father.

Although Aunt Deborah was a Quaker she was sure of the righteousness of America's war against oppression.

"Perhaps I could see my father if I go to visit you, Aunt Deborah," said Ruth hopefully.

But Aunt Deborah could give no assurance as to this. She knew that any day might see Washington's army moving from its winter quarters.

"Thee could help me with the garden," she responded. "The bees will soon be about their work now; and there are many things in the country for a small maid to find pleasure in."

"Did you ever see Lafayette, Aunt Deborah?" Ruth asked.

"Why, child! Did not thy mother tell thee? He stopped at my door one day. He was on horseback, and only two soldiers with him. They had ridden out from camp to make sure no English spies were about, and he stopped to ask for a cup of water. He was pleased to take milk instead. Thee shall see the very cup from which he drank, Ruth. It was one of the pink lustre cups, and I put it apart from the others. Some day thee shall have it for thy own," said Aunt Deborah, smiling at Ruth's evident delight.

As Ruth listened she resolved that nothing should prevent her from visiting Aunt Deborah. Perhaps she might see Lafayette as well as her dear father. Perhaps the young Frenchman might again call at

Aunt Deborah's door, and she, Ruth Pennell, hand him the pink lustre cup filled with milk.

Aunt Deborah's voice interrupted these pleasant day-dreams.

"Now, Ruth, thee may help me wash the dishes; and we will make sure that Hero is safely indoors," she said.

"Yes, indeed. Oh! Aunt Deborah, this has been a splendid day, after all," the little girl responded, thinking of Hero safe at home, of Winifred's visit, and of the pink lustre cup that some day would be her own.

CHAPTER VII

GILBERT'S PLAY

RUTH was up in good season the next morning, and Aunt Deborah was quite willing for her little niece to take Hero for a morning call on Winifred; and it was not yet nine o'clock when Ruth pushed open the gate that led from the alley into the Merrills' garden.

The stable stood beside this gate, and was some distance from the house. Fluff, the pony, had a fine box stall with a window looking into the garden. Fluff belonged to Gilbert; but Gilbert had grown so tall that he thought the pony too small for his use, and on Winifred's last birthday had given her all right and title to the little gray pony, whose thick mane and plume-like tail had made the name "Fluff" most appropriate.

The stable was nearly hidden from the house by shrubs and trees, and Gilbert and Winifred found it a fine play-house. Ruth often wished that there was a stable in her father's garden, and that she had a pony exactly like Fluff.

At the sound of Hero's bark Winifred and Gilbert both appeared in the doorway of the stable, and close behind them stood Betty Hastings. Ruth stood still with a questioning look at Winifred. She was sure that Gilbert had asked Betty to take the part of Lafayette, and for a moment she was tempted to turn away without a word. But before she could act on this impulse there was a chorus of welcoming greetings for her and for Hero, and Winifred came running to meet her.

"Betty is going to take the part of Lord Cornwallis!" Winifred exclaimed, as she put her arm about Ruth and led her to the stable. "Gilbert thinks you were splendid to go straight to General Howe and ask for Hero," she added, "and Betty wants to hear just what Major André said," so Ruth, instead of finding herself entirely supplanted by Betty, as she had for a moment feared, was surrounded by the eager interest and attention of the little group. It seemed to Ruth that she had never before known how nice Betty Hastings really was. The older girl was evidently greatly impressed by the fact that Ruth had sat next to the English General at his dinner table.

"I wish I could have been you, Ruth," she declared admiringly.

"It was all right for Ruth to ask for her dog," Gilbert interrupted, "but *I* wouldn't have sat down at General Howe's table. Not much I wouldn't."

"But Major André lifted me up. I didn't do it myself," replied Ruth, suddenly ashamed that she had entirely forgotten that the English officers were her enemies, and had even been rather pleased that no other little girl in Philadelphia could say that she had sat at the dinner table of the great English General.

"And you are no better than a Tory, Betty Hastings," Gilbert continued, looking disapprovingly toward brown-eyed Betty. "You said a little while ago that you would rather be Lord Cornwallis than Washington."

"Well, what if I did? I only meant in your play; because the English uniform is fine. All scarlet and gold," Betty explained.

She was smiling, and evidently did not care at all if Gilbert did not approve of her. "Come on and tell us what your play is about," she added.

Gilbert's frown vanished. He drew a roll of paper from his pocket; and, looking soberly at his companions, said:

"The name of my play is 'America Defeats the Foe.' It is in two acts. The first act is Lord Cornwallis, that's you, Betty, on his knees asking Washington to spare his life. The second act is Washington and Lafayette and their triumphant army, Winifred is the army, marching into Philadelphia."

"Um-m," said Betty slowly, "what does Washington say when Lord Cornwallis asks him to spare his life?"

"I don't just know yet," Gilbert admitted. "I thought I'd wait until we rehearsed."

"You said Fluff and Hero were to have parts," Winifred reminded him, a little anxiously.

"What does Lafayette wear?" asked Ruth.

Gilbert's face flushed: "Just like girls, wanting to know everything before I've had time to think. But I can tell you one thing, we'll have to plan our costumes now."

"Mine is all planned," said Betty; "you know there is an English officer lodging at our house, and I'll borrow his scarlet coat."

"My Aunt Deborah has seen Lafayette," Ruth announced proudly, "and I'll ask her to tell me just what he wore, and then perhaps I can look just like him."

Winifred said nothing. Gilbert had already told her that he meant to dress up two broom-sticks as American soldiers, and these were to "march" on each side of Winifred, with her aid and assistance. She was always ready to help Gilbert in all his plans, but she was beginning to think that it would be rather a difficult task to be a triumphant army; especially as Gilbert had told her that she must cheer for Washington and Lafayette when they reached the "State House," whose location he had not yet decided on.

"Aren't you going to have any girls or women in your play?" asked Betty, apparently not greatly pleased with Gilbert's brief description. "*I* think you ought to have Lady Washington in a balcony waving her handkerchief, when the victorious army enters Philadelphia. I could be Lady Washington, because I'll be all through being Lord Cornwallis in the first act," and Betty smiled at her companions as if sure they would be greatly pleased by her suggestion.

"Why, yes ——" began Gilbert, but before he could say more a wail from Winifred made them all looks at her in surprise.

"Betty Hastings shan't be everything! If she's going to be Lady Washington I won't play. I won't be an army, anyway," she sobbed.

"Oh! I don't care!" said Betty good-humoredly. "I just happened to think of it, that's all. I'd just as soon be the army."

It was finally decided that Winifred should be Lady Washington, and wave from the top of the grain-bin when the triumphant army passed. Lafayette was to ride on Fluff, and Gilbert said he meant to borrow a horse for George Washington. Hero was to follow the army. It was dinner-time before all these important questions were settled; and it was agreed that they would meet again the next morning for another rehearsal. Gilbert promised to have speeches ready for Lafayette and Cornwallis.

"The way it is now nobody has anything to say but Washington," Betty had said, and Gilbert had agreed that Cornwallis should at least say, "Spare me, noble Washington," while Lafayette could make some response to Washington's speech, which Betty thought far too long, thanking the young Frenchman for his aid to America.

"I wish Gilbert would let you make up our speeches, Betty," said Ruth, looking up at her companion with admiring eyes, as the two girls stopped for a moment at Ruth's door. "It wasn't any play at all until you told him what to do."

"It will come out all right," responded Betty. "It's the dressing up that will be fun. I wish we could get Ned Ferris to play the drum and march ahead."

Ruth agreed that a drummer would make it seem more like a triumphant army.

"Do you suppose the English officer at your house will really lend you his red coat?" questioned Ruth.

Betty laughed. "Of course he will; for he won't know anything about it. 'Tis his best coat, and hangs in a closet in the passage near his room. He wears it only now and then. I shall just borrow it, and then hang it back in the closet," declared Betty. "Just as you did your mother's dress," she added quickly, as if half-afraid of Ruth's disapproval, and with a "good-bye until to-morrow, Lafayette," she ran quickly down the street.

Ruth was a little thoughtful as she went into the house. She wished that she had told Betty that she was sorry about borrowing her mother's dress without permission, and that it would be wiser to ask the soldier to lend his coat. Then she remembered that Betty was nearly thirteen, and of course must know more than a little girl only just past ten.

Aunt Deborah greeted her smilingly. "I have been brushing thy mother's gown, Ruth. 'Twas sadly in need of it, and a tear on the side breadth. But I have mended it so well that 'twill hardly be noticed, and sponged and pressed the dress until it looks as well as ever," she said.

Ruth's face brightened.

"Oh! I am so glad, Aunt Deborah. Then Mother need not know I wore it, or that I went to see General Howe. You will not tell her, will you, Aunt Deborah?" said Ruth eagerly.

The smile faded from Aunt Deborah's face, and she turned away from Ruth with a little sigh.

"No, I will not tell her, Ruth. But thee will surely do that thyself," she answered.

"But you say the dress looks as well as ever," said Ruth, "and, oh, Aunt Deborah! It will make Mother feel so bad to know that I was so thoughtless," and Ruth looked pleadingly toward her aunt.

"Thee shall settle the matter for thyself, Ruth. But I hope thee will tell thy mother," responded Aunt Deborah. But Ruth made no reply.

In the afternoon Winifred came over, and the two little girls sat down on the back porch to talk over Gilbert's play. Winifred said that the broomsticks could be dressed up in some blue coverlets, with cocked hats made from paper, and Ruth promised to help Winifred make the hats.

"Betty is going to borrow her mother's fine silk cape and bonnet for me to wear as Lady Washington," Winifred continued eagerly. "Isn't Betty splendid to let me have the very best part of all, and to get so many nice things for us to dress up in?"

"Will she ask her mother for the cape and bonnet?" Ruth questioned.

Of course she will," declared Winifred, "and I have thought of something. We can dress Josephine and Cecilia in their best dresses, and have them sit beside Lady Washington on the top of the grain box."

Ruth agreed that such a plan would add to the success of Gilbert's play.

"My mother is coming home in a few days," she said when Winifred said that she must go home.

"Well, I guess she will be proud when you tell her that you went to General Howe and made him find Hero," Winifred replied. For Winifred was sure that it had been a very courageous act to face the English General.

"I am not going to tell her a word about it," was Ruth's reply.

CHAPTER VIII

BETTY RUNS AWAY

THE days now passed very quickly for Ruth and her friends. Every day Betty Hastings, Winifred, Ruth and Gilbert were in the Merrills' garden or stable at work on the costumes for "America Conquers the Foe." Ned Ferris, a boy not much older than Ruth, had promised Gilbert to play on his drum, and to march at the head of the "army"; he would not need to rehearse, so would not come until the day decided on for the play. Ned had also offered the loan of his brown pony, a much larger animal than Fluff, for "Washington" to ride; and now Gilbert, Winifred and Ruth were all sure that the play would be a success. Betty Hastings was not so confident. She had begun to fear that it would be no easy matter to borrow the scarlet coat without the owner's knowledge; and she was even more doubtful in regard to her mother's fine cape and bonnet; but she said nothing of this to the others.

If she had known that Gilbert had invited her mother, as well as a number of other friends of Mrs. Merrill's, to what he described as "a birthday surprise for my mother," Betty would doubtless have given up her part; but Gilbert had asked each guest to keep the invitation a secret; and it was probable that a surprise was in store for "Cornwallis" as well as for Gilbert's mother.

Mrs. Pennell returned home from Germantown on the very morning of Mrs. Merrill's birthday, and Ruth was so delighted at her arrival that she nearly forgot to ask her mother to come to the play that afternoon, as Gilbert had requested. Gilbert had said that he wished Mistress Deborah Farleigh would come with Ruth's mother, but added : "It isn't any use to ask her, for Quakers don't believe in plays."

"But this is different; I'm sure she will come," Ruth had responded eagerly; and had been greatly pleased when Aunt Deborah agreed, saying that, "'Twas surely a patriotic lesson that she would like well to see."

Mrs. Pennell also praised Gilbert's cleverness, and promised to be ready in good season. "Perhaps I had best wear my brown silk to do credit to Mrs. Merrill's birthday party," she said, and wondered why Ruth became so silent and looked so sober. For a moment Ruth was tempted to tell her mother the whole story of her visit to General Howe; but she resisted the impulse. "It would spoil everything to make Mother feel bad the very day she has come home," the little girl assured herself; but she no

longer felt light-hearted, and when her mother patted Hero's head, and said that she knew he had
taken good care of everything in her absence, Ruth
grew even more serious.

Aunt Deborah was very quiet; but now and then
her eyes rested on Ruth a little questioningly.

"I suppose Aunt Deborah is thinking I ought to
tell Mother," thought Ruth, and was glad to hurry
away as soon as they finished dinner, saying she
must be in good season, as Gilbert had set three
o'clock as the hour for the arrival of his audience.

"You must come in through the alley," Ruth
reminded her mother and aunt; for Gilbert had
decided that the guests were to be a part of the surprise for his mother.

Gilbert was arranging seats for the company just
inside the door of the stable behind a rope stretched
from the front to the door of Fluff's stall. On the
previous day the children had made an excursion to
Fair Mount, and had brought home a quantity of
blossoming boughs of the white dogwood, branches
of pine, and of flowering elder, and these were used
to make a background for the seats intended for the
guests, to hide a part of the grain-bin, from which
Lady Washington was to wave, and made the stable
a very attractive and pleasant place. The guests
could look through the open door into the garden

where blue iris, yellow daffodils and purple lilacs were already in bloom.

When Ruth came running to the stable Winifred called out to her from the top of the grain-bin: "Look, Ruth! Look!" and Ruth stopped in the doorway with an exclamation of surprise. For there was Winifred wearing Mrs. Hastings' beautiful blue mantle of rich silk, and a bonnet with soft blue plumes, and beside her sat two other figures that, for a moment, Ruth believed to be two strange ladies. Then she realized that Winifred had "dressed up" bundles of hay in two old gowns of her mother's, with their "heads" crowned by wreaths of leaves and flowers.

Winifred laughed delightedly at Ruth's astonishment. "You see, Josephine and Cecilia were not tall enough; and of course Lady Washington ought to have company," she explained.

Gilbert, dressed in a blue coat, yellow knee-breeches, and with a crimson and white scarf pinned across his coat, came to the door. He wore a cocked hat, and a wooden sword was fastened at his side, and he endeavored to stand as tall as possible.

"Betty is waiting for you behind the lilac bushes," he said, and vanished; and Ruth ran off to the bunch of lilacs behind the stable where Betty, in a scarlet coat that covered her completely, was holding Fluff's bridle-rein, and close by stood Ned Ferris beside his brown pony.

"Here is your coat and hat, 'Lafayette,' " said Betty, pointing to a bundle which Ruth hastened to open.

The coat was of blue velvet. It was one that Betty had found in a trunk in her mother's attic. There were ruffles of yellowed lace at the wrists, and tarnished gilt buttons and braid on the shoulders. This old velvet coat had belonged to Betty's grandfather, and was highly valued by her father. But Betty had not asked permission to take it.

Ruth tied up her hair and put on the cocked hat that she had helped Winifred make; then with Betty's aid she slipped on the velvet coat, and with the addition of a wooden sword which Gilbert had made for her she was ready for her part in the play.

The guests all arrived in good season, and were escorted to their seats by "Washington" himself, who then ran to the house to announce to his mother that some friends of hers were in the garden.

Mrs. Merrill, greatly to Gilbert's satisfaction, did not seem to notice that he was not dressed as usual, and walked beside him down the garden path; as a turn in the path brought them in sight of the stable door Gilbert said:

"This is a birthday surprise for you, Mother. It's a play, and here is the programme," and he handed her a strip of white paper bordered with a row of stars cut from gilt paper. At the top Gilbert had printed:

"AMERICA CONQUERS THE FOE"

A Play
by
Gilbert Merrill
For Mother's Birthday

ACT FIRST
Cornwallis Begs For Mercy
Cornwallis- - - - - - - B. Hastings
Washington - - - - - - G. Merrill

ACT SECOND
Washington's Triumphant Army Enters
Philadelphia
Washington - - - - - - G. Merrill
Lafayette - - - - - - - R. Pennell
Lady Washington - - Miss Winifred Merrill
Army
Band.

Mrs. Merrill read the program me admiringly.

"It is indeed a wonderful birthday surprise, my dear boy," she said smilingly, "and I am proud of you," and she hurried forward to greet and welcome her friends, while Gilbert ran to summon "Cornwallis" to be ready for the first act.

An old horse-blanket, suspended from the hay-loft in the rear of the stable, served as a curtain behind which knelt Betty in the scarlet coat. Gilbert now took his place beside her, trying to look stern and noble. At Gilbert's whistle Winifred, who was in the hay-loft, was to pull up the blanket by the long strings that Gilbert had skilfully arranged.

The whistle sounded clearly. Up rose the curtain. There was an approving murmur from the audience at the sight of "Cornwallis" on his knees.

"Spare me, noble Washington!" said Betty, but in rather a feeble voice.

Washington's right hand was stretched over the head of his conquered foe.

"Arise, Cornwallis. Flee for your life. My army is at hand," responded Washington; and Betty, stumbling a little, escaped from the rear door, while Washington marched out to meet his army, and the audience applauded.

Betty's mother had noticed the red coat, and wondered what English soldier had consented to lend it for such a purpose. It did not occur to her that Betty had taken it from their lodger's closet.

When Betty had entered the stable by the rear door and knelt according to Washington's directions she could hear the murmur of voices.

"Who is with your mother?" she whispered to "Washington," but there had been no time to answer, and Betty found herself facing not only Gilbert's mother but a dozen other ladies of whom her mother was one; and it was a very anxious and troubled Betty who joined the little group behind the lilac bushes and, slipping off the red coat, put on an old coat and hat belonging to Gilbert's father, and with the dressed up broomsticks, took her place behind Fluff as the "Army."

Ned Ferris sounded a measured "rat-a-tat-tat" on his drum and strode toward the entrance to the stable, followed by Washington and Lafayette, the "Army," and the docile Hero. Lady Washington scrambled from the hay-loft to the top of the grain-bin, drew her fine silk mantle about her, and smiled graciously down upon the assembled guests. Mrs. Hastings looked up at her. "For pity's sake!" her seatmate heard her murmur, "my best mantle and bonnet!" But at that moment came the quick beat of a drum.

Washington's pony, a little annoyed and nervous, and Fluff, determined to reach his stall as quickly as possible, although "Lafayette" endeavored to guide him in the appointed course, entered the stable.

"Washington" drew rein beneath the grain-bin and lifted his hat to Lady Washington, who leaned forward to wave in response; but unfortunately her bonnet strings were not fastened, and the fine bonnet with its blue plumes fell from her head and went tumbling down almost on Hero's brown head. In a second the dog had seized it, and forgetting his part in the procession, jumped this way and that, shaking this new plaything with delighted satisfaction.

Mrs. Hastings kept her seat resolutely. It would have been an easy matter to have stepped from her seat and rescued the bonnet. But Mrs. Hastings knew that such a movement on her part would have brought Gilbert's play to an untimely end, and spoiled the pleasure of all the guests, as well as of the children who took part. So she did not move, even when Hero fled out into the garden with the plumes grasped in his teeth. Betty, Ruth and Winifred never forgot that moment, nor the fact that Mrs. Hastings had apparently not seen what happened. Even in her fright at the results of her "borrowing" Betty Hastings was very proud of her mother.

The drummer played on. The two ponies were swung around face to face; Washington and Lafayette clasped hands for a moment; then side by side, with drum playing, but with a silent army, the little procession vanished through the rear door.

Gilbert was delighted with his success. It seemed to him that everything had gone very well, and he was especially grateful to Betty Hastings for securing the English officer's coat.

But Betty, having seen the ruin of the bonnet, had suddenly realized that it was a serious matter to take the belongings of other people without their permission; and her first thought was of the officer's coat. Whatever happened she must return that coat to the closet from which she had taken it as soon as possible. Then she would try and explain to her mother that she had not meant any harm should befall the borrowed articles. So, grasping the red coat, Betty opened the door into the alley and started off as fast as she could go; while Ruth, still wearing the fine velvet coat, crouched down behind the lilac bushes, too unhappy to care if the play had been a success or not; for as "Lafayette" faced the audience she had seen that her mother was wearing the brown silk dress.

CHAPTER IX

BETTY'S ADVENTURE

"Come, Ruth, Mistress Hastings is waiting for thy fine velvet coat," and Ruth looked up to see Aunt Deborah smiling down upon her; and in a moment the little girl was clinging to Aunt Deborah's arm, and asking anxiously:

"Did Mother find the mended place in her dress? Oh, Aunt Deborah! I do wish I had told her all about it!"

"Slip off the coat, dear child, and run and tell her now," said Aunt Deborah, and in a moment Ruth was running across the garden to where her mother was standing with Mrs. Merrill. Mrs. Pennell smiled down at her little daughter, and clasping the warm little hand in her own turned toward the gate.

In a moment Ruth was in the midst of her story, and Mrs. Pennell listened without a word until Ruth, breathless and almost in tears, finished by saying:

"I didn't think it would hurt the dress, Mother! I'm so sorry. And I am sorry I didn't tell you the moment you got home."

Ruth felt her hand clasped a little more closely at this; but her mother made no response until they were in Ruth's pleasant chamber. Then Mrs. Pennell drew her little girl down beside her on the broad window-seat; and leaning her head against her mother's shoulder Ruth told of the day she had stayed upstairs as a punishment for her thoughtlessness.

"Mother, you haven't said a word!" Ruth finally exclaimed, looking up anxiously. "Are you ashamed of me?"

"Why, I think I am rather proud of my little daughter," was the smiling response. "You set your own punishment, and I know you will stop and think when next you plan such a masquerade party. My dress, it seems, is but little the worse, after all; and Hero is well worth some sacrifice. Perhaps if you had not been 'dressed up' you would not have been admitted to General Howe's house, and might not have succeeded in rescuing Hero," said Mrs. Pennell, stooping down to kiss her little girl's flushed cheek.

"Oh, Mother! I do love you," exclaimed the happy child. "I'll never be afraid to tell you everything."

"Of course you will tell me everything. That is what mothers are for," rejoined Mrs. Pennell. "And now I will take off my silk gown, and you had best smooth your hair and make yourself tidy for supper."

"That sounds like Aunt Deborah," said Ruth laughingly. But as she obeyed her mother's suggestion she thought happily that now Mother was at home everything was sure to go smoothly.

When Gilbert's play was over Mrs. Hastings, although sadly troubled over Betty's "borrowings," and the ruin of her pretty bonnet, complimented Gilbert and Winifred on the success of the play; and not until she had chatted for a few moments with Mrs. Merrill did she go to rescue her valued mantle and the treasured velvet coat. She hoped the English officer's coat was none the worse for its part in the play; and, like Betty, she hoped to return it before it was missed by its rightful owner; for it would be no easy matter to explain why it had been borrowed, and she knew its loss would make serious trouble.

She noticed that her mantle was dusty and wrinkled, and that the lace on the velvet coat was torn. The scarlet coat, however, was not to be found, and Betty had also disappeared.

Deciding that she would find her little daughter and the coat safely at home Mrs. Hastings bade her friends good-bye and started for her walk home. But she did not find Betty there. Supper time came, and still no Betty. A servant was sent to Mrs. Merrill's to inquire for the little girl, but came hurrying back with the tidings that Betty had not been seen since the end of the play.

Mrs. Merrill now looked through every room, but Betty was not to be found. She inquired at the homes of her neighbors, but no one had seen the little girl.

The April twilight deepened to dusk; the stars shone out and found Mrs. Hastings anxious and troubled, for she could find no trace of Betty.

When Betty ran down the alley she had thought it would be an easy matter to reach home with the red coat; but she had forgotten that Philadelphia was full of the King's soldiers, and that a bareheaded little girl racing down the street with the coat of an English officer over her arm would not escape notice; and she had only reached Second Street when a passing soldier called to her. His call only made her run the faster, and the soldier sped after her. If Betty had stopped at once, told her own name and address, and the name of the owner of the coat, the soldier would doubtless have taken her directly home and made sure that she had told him the truth, and it is probable that her troubles would have been at an end. But Betty was now too frightened to think clearly. She did not even know the direction in which she ran was straight away from her home. The English soldier ran clumsily, and Betty, turning quickly into another street, soon distanced him; but only to run straight into another soldier, who seized her firmly by both arms, swung her about, and without a word marched her down the street.

"Making off with an officer's coat," he said, after what seemed a very long time to the frightened girl. "What's your name?"

Betty made no response. She resolved that no one should ever know that Betty Hastings had been suspected of such a dreadful thing as taking what she had no right to take.

"Won't speak, eh? Well, I'll take you to Captain De Lancy and see what he has to say to you," said the soldier, and the silent little girl, still holding the scarlet coat, was led down one street after another until she saw the shining waters of the Schuylkill River before her, and the soldier led her up the steps of an old stone house whose garden ran down to the river. The soldier was evidently familiar with the house, for he pushed open the door and led Betty into a big pleasant room, and motioned toward a comfortable chair.

"You can sit there until the captain comes in; and you had best tell me your name. 'Twill do you no good to sulk," he said, taking the coat from her reluctant grasp. But Betty only set her lips more firmly. She resolved not to speak, no matter what might befall her.

"Very well, Miss. I'll leave you to find your tongue," said the soldier, laying the coat carefully over a chair and leaving the room. Betty heard him turn the key in the lock. She was tired, and leaned back in the cushioned chair, hardly realizing what had befallen her. She could hear steps now and then outside the door, and every moment expected that it would open and the captain of whom the soldier had spoken would appear.

But the room grew shadowy in the deepening twilight and no one came near. Betty's thoughts flew homeward to the candle-lit dining-room where Dinah, the Hastings' colored servant, would be spreading the table for supper, and Betty realized that she was very hungry.

She left her seat and tiptoed toward a long window at the further end of the room. The window looked out into the garden, and Betty instantly realized that it swung in on hinges and was not fastened, and that it would be an easy matter to let herself down to the ground.

"I must take the coat," she thought, and crept back to the chair where the scarlet coat lay. In a moment she was back at the window and had dropped the coat to the ground; and now, grasping the window sill with both hands, she let herself carefully down. Picking up the coat, and keeping close in the shadow of the house, Betty made her way until she was near the door through which she had entered the house. She went very carefully, peering ahead into the shadows, and listening intently for any sound that might warn her that her flight had been discovered. But she heard no sound, and at last she reached the road.

"It is too dark for any one to know what color the coat is now," she thought, as she hurried along.

Betty realized that she was a long distance from home, but she was sure that she could soon find her way to some familiar street and then it would be an easy matter to reach home. Now and then she passed groups of people homeward bound, or English soldiers sauntering along the street, and then turning a corner she gave a little exclamation of delight, for there, close at hand, were the brick walls of Christ Church, its graceful spire rising against the clear April sky. And now home was near at hand and Betty quickened her pace. She had almost forgotten her mother's ruined bonnet and the fact that she had no excuse to give for borrowing the things for Gilbert's play without permission. All she could think of was the fact that she was in sight of home. She ran up the steps and the door opened as if by magic, and Betty's mother clasped her little girl, scarlet coat and all, in her welcoming arms.

CHAPTER X

THE LOST PROGRAMME

THE scarlet coat, after being carefully brushed and pressed, was returned to its place in the closet; and its owner never knew or imagined the part it had taken in Gilbert's play. The soldier who had locked Betty into Captain De Lancy's room, and returned to find that the silent little captive had outwitted him and made her escape, decided that it was best to keep the affair to himself, and say nothing about a little girl with an officer's coat for which she would not account.

Ruth and Winifred came early the next morning to make sure that Betty was safe at home, and listened eagerly to the story of her adventure.

"Do you suppose you could find the way back to the stone house?" questioned Ruth.

"Yes, I am sure I could," responded Betty; but she did not suggest, as Ruth hoped, that they should all make an excursion to the house by the river. In fact, Winifred and Ruth both agreed on their way home that Betty seemed very sober. And it was true that Betty was more quiet than usual for several days; for she realized that she had had a narrow escape from a serious punishment. Nor could she forget the pretty plumed bonnet that Hero had so gaily destroyed. The fact that her mother did not speak of the bonnet only made Betty the more repentant. She and Ruth had both resolved that they would not again take for granted that they could use other people's property without permission.

"Aunt Deborah is going home to Barren Hill to-morrow," said Ruth, as she and Winifred came near home; "Farmer Withely is to call for her. You know he brings in butter and cheese from his farm every Thursday, and Aunt Deborah will ride home in his wagon. I wish I were going with her."

"Oh, Ruth Pennell!" said Winifred reproachfully.

"Well, I do. Barren Hill is half-way to Valley Forge, and perhaps I could see my father. And, Winifred! One day Lafayette stopped at Aunt Deborah's door! Perhaps I might see him; perhaps he might ask me to carry a message for him," said Ruth eagerly.

"Little girls can't carry war messages," Winifred rejoined confidently. "You are just like Gilbert, always wishing you could do something for Lafayette. I don't see why. I would rather help Washington."

"It's because Lafayette came 'way from France," Ruth replied, "and, anyway, I am going to Barren Hill. Mother says that I may go next month."

"I have thought of something!" Winifred announced. "To-morrow you and I will drive out a little

IT WAS A FAVORITE PLAY-HOUSE

way with your aunt. With Fluff, I mean; and Hero
may go too. I will harness Fluff onto the cart, and we
will be all ready to start at the same time they do."

Ruth agreed that this would be a fine plan, and
both the girls were sure that Aunt Deborah would be
pleased that they wished to go a part of the way
with her. They decided to take "Josephine" and
"Cecilia," as well as Hero, with them.

"It will make up to them for not taking part in the
play," said Winifred. So much had happened during
the past week that Ruth had entirely forgotten the
unfinished chair for Cecilia, but now she spoke of it
to Winifred.

"I will help you finish it. But let's take our dolls
and work into the garden; it is too warm to stay in
the house," she said, and in a short time the two little girls had brought Cecilia and Josephine, as well
as their sewing bags, to the shade of the wide-
spreading maple tree that grew in the further corner of the Pennells' garden. Ruth's father had built
a low seat around this tree, and it was a favorite
play-house for the two little friends. Hero followed
them, and stretched himself out at their feet, quite
sure that they were both happier because of his
presence.

For a little while the girls worked steadily, cover-
ing with chintz the cardboard pieces that would
form the chair.

"I'll put it together," said Winifred, and with skilful fingers she fastened the seat, back and arms; and with a triumphant "There!" set it down beside Ruth, who looked at it admiringly, and lost no time in establishing Cecilia in her new possession.

"Wouldn't it be fine if we could make a sofa, and a table and a little bed for each of our dolls?" suggested Ruth.

"We can," declared Winifred, "but I think it would be nicer to have the table and bed made of wood. Let's go in your shed and see if we can find some nice smooth pieces."

"And Father's tool box is in the shed," said Ruth, as they left their dolls in Hero's care and ran across the garden to the shed, whose open door faced the big maple.

The shed was nearly square. Beside the wide door there were two windows, both looking into the garden, and beneath these was Mr. Pennell's workbench, and a box containing his treasured tools; and on a long shelf over the bench were carefully arranged strips and squares of polished wood. For in the days of peace Mr. Pennell had used his leisure hours in making frames for pictures, a work-box, desk or light-stand; and had collected this store of material from many sources. Ruth had often played about in the shed while her father was at work, but she had no idea of the value of his store of wood.

"Oh, Winifred! Look! This will make a fine table!" she said, standing on the work-bench and pulling down a strip of curly maple.

"And here are some dark shiny strips, just the thing for bed-posts!" said Winnie, drawing out a slender length of highly polished mahogany. In a few minutes the two girls had pulled down a number of strips of wood, had opened Mr. Pennell's tool-chest and taken out a number of planes, a small saw, gimlets and a hammer.

"But we haven't any patterns," said Winifred. "You know we had a pattern for the chair."

"We don't need any pattern for a table. It is just a top and four legs, one at each corner," declared Ruth. "We can begin on the table to-day; then we can look at sofas and beds and make patterns, if we need to."

"Here is something to measure with," said Winifred, holding up a foot-rule. "We can make anything! Oh, Ruth! Instead of making doll furniture let's make truly tables. I am sure some of those pieces are large enough."

"Winifred, you always think of just the right thing," Ruth responded admiringly. "Let's make a table for a present for Betty. She got all those nice things for us to dress up in, and we have never made her a present."

Winifred nodded approvingly. She was greatly pleased by Ruth's admiration, and she thought that

Betty would be greatly surprised to discover that two girls so much younger than herself could really make a table.

"Ruth! Ruth!" called Aunt Deborah from the back porch. "Dinner is ready!"

So the two little girls were obliged to leave their pleasant plans, and, after promising to return early that afternoon, Winifred started for home while Ruth ran into the house.

"My chair is all finished for Cecilia," she announced as she took her seat at the dinner-table, "and Winifred and I are going to make a table for Betty."

Mrs. Pennell and Aunt Deborah both smiled their approval, thinking that the table for Betty, like Cecilia's chair, was to be made of paste-board.

"Thee must bring thy doll to Barren Hill," said Aunt Deborah. "There are fine places to play in the big barn and in the pine woods, and thy doll will be company for thee."

"How soon may I visit Aunt Deborah, Mother?" Ruth asked eagerly. "May I not go with Farmer Withely next week?"

"I cannot spare you so soon, Ruthie dear," responded her mother, "and I will have to ask permission from the English General for you to leave the town. You see they fear even small Americans," she concluded laughingly. But before dinner was over it was decided that, if all went well, Ruth should go to Barren Hill about the first of May. That seemed a long time to Ruth; but she remembered that Betty's table was not even begun, and if she and Winifred did decide to make furniture for their dolls the three weeks that must pass before her visit to Barren Hill would perhaps be none too long a time.

Mrs. Pennell had just left the table when there was a rap at the door, and before any one could respond it opened, and there stood Winifred; her face was pale and she was evidently frightened.

"Oh, Mrs. Pennell! There are two English officers at our house. They have come to take Gilbert," she exclaimed, "and they want Ruth too."

" 'Take Gilbert'!" echoed Mrs. Pennell. "What has he done? And what do they want of Ruth?"

"Oh! It's because of the play. Mother lost the programme we made for her. It blew away, and an English soldier found it; and they are going to take Ruth too," Winifred finished nearly in tears.

"I will go and speak with these officers," said Aunt Deborah calmly. "Thee need not be troubled, Winifred. Thee and Ruth had best come with me so they can see how dangerous an enemy they have to arrest," and Aunt Deborah smiled so reassuringly that Winifred took courage, and followed Aunt Deborah to the door. They were soon in the Merrills' garden, just in time to meet two English soldiers with Gilbert between them coming down the steps.

Aunt Deborah went forward smilingly.

"Thee does not mean to take this lad from his home," she said, speaking to the elder of the two men. "He has done nothing worthy of thy notice, and his mother can ill spare him."

"That may be, madam. But we must obey orders. We have to take G. Merrill and R. Pennell to General Howe," the man answered civilly.

"Here is R. Pennell," said Aunt Deborah, her hand resting protectingly on Ruth's shoulder. "Surely thee does not mean to take this little girl?"

The soldiers seemed somewhat surprised at this, but repeated that they must obey orders. Gilbert did not seem at all afraid; he took Ruth by the hand, and told her that it was nothing to be alarmed about. Mrs. Merrill, Aunt Deborah, Ruth's mother and Winifred kept close to the "prisoners" as the little party made its way down the street toward the headquarters of the English General.

CHAPTER XI

A LONG ROAD

"WHAT is this?" called a pleasant voice, and the two soldiers halted instantly and saluted a young officer who blocked their way.

"If thee please, sir, there has been a mistake made," said Aunt Deborah, and proceeded to tell the story of the birthday entertainment that the children had given for Mrs. Merrill.

The young officer listened gravely.

"As you say, madam, they are but children; but such games find little favor among loyal English people," he responded.

"But thee must remember we are Americans," said Aunt Deborah fearlessly. The young officer turned and walked beside them. Now and then he smiled as if amused by his own thoughts, but he said nothing more until they reached the headquarters of the General.

"Wait here a moment," he said, and ran up the steps.

"I shall tell them that Ruth had nothing to do with it, and that I am the only one to blame," Gilbert said to Mrs. Pennell. "Of course they won't punish any one but me."

Before Mrs. Pennell could reply the young officer appeared at the door, and came slowly down the steps.

"Come with me, young sir," he said, resting his hand on Gilbert's shoulder. "You may take the little girls home, ladies," he added. "I am quite sure they will not prove a danger to England's cause."

"I will wait for my son," said Mrs. Merrill. "I do not suppose you mean to detain him long."

"I cannot say as to that, madam; but you are quite welcome to wait. If you will come in I will see that you find a comfortable chair," he replied courteously.

"I will wait here," said Mrs. Merrill.

"And we will wait also," declared Ruth's mother.

Ruth and Winifred clasped each other's hands as they watched Gilbert being led up the steps. They thought their mothers were very brave indeed to reply so calmly to an English officer. Gilbert was absent not more than a half hour, but it seemed much longer to the anxious little group. He came down the steps alone, and when his mother slipped her hand under one arm while Winifred clasped his other hand he smiled and said: "Humph! All they did was laugh and tell me to choose a better plot for my next play. They are not soldiers at all. Why, they asked me if I would not like to take a part in one of Major André's plays."

"What did you say, Gilbert?" questioned Winifred.

"I said '*No*.' And that's all I said. And I did not thank them for the offer; and then they laughed more than ever. I wish Washington would drive them out of Philadelphia," answered Gilbert, who was a trifle disappointed that the Englishmen had not taken his play more seriously. He would not have minded if he had been held as a prisoner for a few days; it would have made him feel that he had really done something to prove his loyalty to the American cause.

But Mrs. Merrill was very glad to have her tall son safely beside her, although she was inclined to agree with him that the gay young English officers took their duties too lightly. There had been balls at the City Tavern every week during the winter, and most of the officers seemed to forget that there were dangers in store for them from the American Army at Valley Forge.

Gilbert's adventure made Ruth and Winifred completely forget their plan to make a table as a present for Betty until late that afternoon; and then they decided not to begin it until after Aunt Deborah's departure the next day.

"Mother has a table shaped like a heart. We could mark a heart on that square piece of dark wood with chalk and then cut it out," suggested Winnie. "I am sure Betty would like that better than a plain square table."

"Of course she would," agreed Ruth. Neither of the little girls realized how hard an undertaking it would be to carve a heart-shaped table top from the square piece of mahogany.

Ruth was awake at an early hour the next morning. The April sun shone warmly in through her open window; the robins, who had built a nest in the hawthorn tree, sang jubilantly as if rejoicing that spring was really at hand, and Ruth could hear her mother and Aunt Deborah moving about in the lower rooms. It was just the day for a ride in the country.

Ruth was glad that Winifred had thought of so pleasant a plan as driving a part of the way with Aunt Deborah. Both the little girls had taken it for granted that their mothers would have no objection. Winifred was used to driving the pony, and had often taken Ruth with her, but they had never been farther than Fair Mount, a pleasant hill just outside the town on the Schuylkill River, or along the quiet streets of the town; but to-day Winifred had said that they would drive until Aunt Deborah should tell them to turn toward home.

Farmer Withely usually arrived in the city at an early hour, delivered his produce, then gave the big brown horse an hour or two rest, and was ready to start on his return journey directly after dinner.

Aunt Deborah did not keep him waiting, and was at the gate with Mrs. Pennell beside her when the round-faced smiling farmer in his long coat of heavy blue drilling and his wide-rimmed hat came driving up.

"Where can Ruth be?" her mother said anxiously, as the farmer lifted Aunt Deborah's trunk into the back of the wagon and stood waiting to help her mount to the high seat.

At that moment the pony carriage drew up behind the wagon with Winnie and Ruth smiling and waving their hands at Aunt Deborah.

"We are going a little way with you, Mistress Farleigh," called Winifred.

"May I go, Mother?" Ruth added.

Aunt Deborah was evidently greatly pleased that the little girls had wished to go a little way with her on her journey home, and Mrs. Pennell smiled and nodded her consent, thinking that Ruth would be safely back in an hour at the longest, and waving her good-byes as Farmer Withely climbed to his seat and the brown horse trotted off, closely followed by Fluff.

Down the street they went, turning now into the broader highway and at last reaching the river road that led straight to Matson's Ford, beyond which the road led on to Valley Forge.

As they came in sight of the river the big horse stopped, and in a moment Fluff was beside the farmer's cart. Aunt Deborah smiled down at the little girls.

" 'Tis best that thee turn toward home now. And I thank thee both for coming so far with me. 'Twill not be long now, Ruth, before I hope to see thee at Barren Hill. And thee, Winifred, will be welcome also whenever thou canst give me the pleasure of a visit."

Before Aunt Deborah had finished speaking Ruth was out of the pony carriage and standing on the step of Farmer Withely's cart holding up a package.

"Here is something I made for you, Aunt Deborah," she said. Aunt Deborah reached down and received the small carefully wrapped package.

"Thank thee, dear child," she said, and Ruth stood by the roadside and waved a good-bye as the brown horse trotted off at a more rapid pace than he had traveled through the town.

"I wish we could have gone farther," she said regretfully as she went back to her seat beside Winifred.

"Well, we can. We'll turn up that shady road and see where it goes," responded Winifred. "What did you give your aunt?"

"A needle-book. Mother helped me make it. It is of blue flannel, with embroidered edges, and shaped like a small book, with Aunt Deborah's initials on the cover," said Ruth. "Would it not be pleasant if you could visit Aunt Deborah when I do?"

Winifred feared that such a visit would not be possible. But the two little friends talked of many things as Fluff trotted along the narrow country road, hardly more than a lane, and sheltered by closely growing trees. Now and then the road came out into an open space, and there would be many violets growing close to the roadside. Then the girls sprang from the cart and gathered handfuls of the fragrant blossoms, while Fluff nibbled at the grass, or twisted his head to watch his young mistress. The wild honeysuckle was also in bloom along a sloping pasture, and Ruth was eager to gather it to take home to her mother. She climbed up the rough slope, followed by Winifred, and they soon had large bunches of the delicate blossoms. From the top of the little hill that they had climbed they could see the distant line of the blue river, and after roaming about for a time they decided it was time to return to Fluff and start for home. The pony whinnied a little impatiently and shook his head at them as they approached.

"He thinks we have stayed too long," said Winifred laughingly. "What time do you suppose it is, Ruth?"

"Oh! we can't have been away from home more than an hour," said Ruth; "but the sky looks cloudy, doesn't it?"

But it was not clouds that made the sky darken, it was the rapidly approaching twilight. The tall trees shut out the golden spring sunshine; and the afternoon had passed so pleasantly that neither Ruth nor Winifred had any idea that evening was close at hand, or that they were miles from home in a solitary and unknown road that had seemed to grow more narrow as they went on.

"Perhaps we had better turn around now," suggested Winifred a few moments after they had gathered the wild honeysuckle. "I told Mother we would be home early. Why, what is the matter with Fluff?" she added in a startled tone, for the little pony had come to a full stop.

Both the little girls jumped out of the cart and ran to the pony's head, which drooped low. Fluff was breathing heavily, and it seemed to Winifred as if his slender legs trembled.

"Why, he can't be tired. He'd that long rest just now," said Ruth anxiously. Neither of them realized that ever since leaving the river the road had run steadily up-hill, or that the pony had been traveling for a number of hours. Fluff was no longer young, and he had never been required to go long distances; and now he could go no further.

"I'll take off his harness," said Winifred quickly. "I hope he isn't going to have a fit. Ned Ferris's pony has fits." It did not take her long to set Fluff free from the pony-cart, and he turned a grateful look toward his little mistress, who began to wish there was a brook or spring near at hand where the little creature could drink.

Ruth smoothed Fluff's head, and Winifred with a bunch of wayside grass rubbed his back and legs.

"He's going to lie down," said Winifred as Fluff moved his head about quickly; and in a moment the tired little creature had stretched himself at their feet.

"What shall we do? I am sure Fluff can't take us home," exclaimed Winifred, "and we can't go and leave him here."

"It can't be very far from home," responded Ruth. "I could go home and tell Gilbert, and he would come right back for you with Ned's pony."

"But what could we do with Fluff?" asked Winifred a little despondently. "He is too tired to drive home."

"Perhaps he'd be rested enough by that time to go home, if he didn't have to pull the cart," said Ruth; "anyway, I do think one of us ought to go home or our mothers will think some harm has befallen us. I'll stay, if you would rather go."

But Winifred shook her head. She did not wish to leave the pony; neither was she pleased at the thought of staying by herself on that lonely road. At last, however, they decided that Ruth's plan was the best they could think of, and Ruth started.

"I'll hurry all the way, Winifred; and Gilbert will come back as fast as he can," she called as she started to run down the hill.

CHAPTER XII

A LONG RIDE

"I WISH we had brought Hero," thought Ruth regretfully as she hurried down the shadowy road, "then he could have come with me for company." For at the last moment before leaving home the little girls had decided that it was not best to let Hero accompany them. There was not room for him in the pony-cart, and for him to race along the streets might well mean that he would again disappear; so Ruth had been quite ready to leave him at home. But now she would have been very glad to have him running along beside her. "Josephine" and "Cecilia" had also been left behind; in fact neither Winifred nor Ruth had remembered the dolls until after they had said good-bye to Aunt Deborah. And, while Ruth was regretting the absence of Hero, Winifred, sitting close beside Fluff, was wishing that her beloved Josephine was there to keep her company.

"It would be a great adventure for Josephine," she thought, looking up through the overhanging branches of the big oak under which Fluff had stopped to rest. For a time she amused herself by braiding the long grass and weaving it about green twigs broken from an elder-bush until she had made a wide, shallow basket with a handle. Into this she put the violets and wild honeysuckle, resolving to take it home as a present to her mother. She put it carefully under the seat of the pony-cart, and then decided to search for a spring or brook, for she was thirsty.

Fluff showed no signs of wishing to start for home, or even to eat the tempting young grass growing near.

"If I find a brook perhaps I can lead him, and then he will get a good drink," thought Winifred, crossing the narrow road and pushing aside a thick growth of wild shrubs.

"Oh!" she exclaimed, for she had stepped at once on to damp yielding moss which covered her low cut slippers and wetted her feet as completely as if she had stepped into a brook. Just beyond this moss lay a clear little pool of water, evidently fed by springs.

Winifred discovered that the farther, or upper, bank of the pool was dry and sandy, and in a few moments she was kneeling beside the clear water and drinking thirstily. She then made her way back to the road, breaking down branches of the shrubs to make a way for Fluff, who was now on his feet looking about as if in search of his little mistress.

"Come on, Fluff," she said coaxingly, grasping the plume-like mane. "Come and have a drink." The pony moved forward obediently. He hesitated a moment at having to push his way through the undergrowth, but with Winifred encouraging and urging him forward he was soon in sight of the pool, and then sprang forward so suddenly that his mane slid through Winifred's hands and she found herself on her hands and knees while Fluff, with his nose in the clear water, was drinking thirstily.

Winifred laughed as she scrambled to her feet. Her shoes and stockings were wet and muddy, her pretty blue linen dress was torn, and now she realized that her hat was gone, that she must have lost it in pushing her way through the undergrowth; but these things seemed of small consequence to Winifred just then; for the pony, with his forefeet planted firmly in the shallow water, was evidently more himself than he had been since he had stopped short under the oak tree.

"I'll lead him back and harness him into the cart and start after Ruth," thought his little mistress happily, "and I do believe it is getting dark!" she added aloud, realizing that the woods seemed very shadowy, as she made her way toward the pool.

As she came near Fluff he lifted his bead from the water, shook himself much as a big dog would do, and whinnied with satisfaction. But as Winifred approached more closely he gave a little dancing step into the water just beyond her reach.

"Oh, Fluff! It isn't any time to play games. We must start for home before it is really dark," said Winifred. But Fluff was now rested, and free from his harness in a fragrant shadowy wood. He was sure that his little mistress must be as ready as himself for a game, so he edged along the pool until a clear space opened before him, and then he stepped out, and trotted briskly away between the tall trees.

"Fluff! Fluff!" called Winifred, running after him. "Oh! where did he go?" for the pony had disappeared as if the earth had swallowed him. Winifred ran on until her way was blocked by thickly growing underbrush. Then she turned back, but now she could not find the pool. The shadows deepened; she could hardly distinguish one tree from another, and there was no sound or sign from the gray pony.

"What shall I do?" she said, standing close to the trunk of a pine tree that rose straight and tall with wide-spreading branches. She realized that she must now be some distance from the road and the big oak tree where she had left the pony-cart, and Fluff perhaps was deep in this wilderness, unable to make his way back; and, worst of all, night was close upon her.

It was indeed a dangerous position for a little girl to be alone in a wilderness as Winifred found herself. It was a time when many wild beasts still wandered about, often coming near to the outskirts of towns and villages. Winifred remembered that only a few weeks earlier a catamount had been killed at Fair Mount, and she knew that in the early spring bears left the dens where they had slept through the winter, and wandered through the woods eating the tender young buds and leaves. She crouched closer to the tree as she remembered these things, and then suddenly she recalled the words that she had worked on her sampler: "There shall no evil befall thee. For he shall give his angels charge over thee, to keep thee in all thy ways."

Her mother had traced the words, and Winifred had worked them in dull blue yarns on the perforated wool cloth. She said them over aloud: "No evil befall thee," and was no longer afraid. She did not think now of the beasts of the dark wood, but of a kindly presence that would shelter her.

"Perhaps Fluff will come and find me," she thought hopefully. "Anyway, Ruth will soon be back with Gilbert, and they will call my name, and I shall call back," and so comforted and encouraged Winifred sat down on the soft pine spills and leaned back against the tall tree. A pair of squirrels chattered noisily in the branches; a soft-footed little animal sped by almost touching her feet, and she could hear faint calls from nesting birds near at hand.

"For he shall give his angels charge over thee," the little girl whispered to herself, and soothed and quieted by the spring fragrance of the wood her eyes closed.

Ruth, meanwhile, was trudging along the road toward home. She was sure that she could find the way without any trouble.

"All I have to do is to turn when I come to the river road and follow it straight back to the city, and then any one can tell me how to get home," she thought, hopefully. But she began to think she should never reach the river road. Her thin shoes were scrubbed and dusty, and she wondered what Aunt Deborah would say at her untidy appearance.

Now and then she would quicken her pace and run until she was out of breath. She began to understand why Fluff was tired out. Just before she reached the river road there was the sound of breaking twigs, and of some animal making its way through the woods, and the next moment a deer followed by a young fawn sprang into the road directly in front of the surprised and startled little girl; but they vanished before Ruth realized that they had been within reach of her hand.

"Oh! I wish Winifred could have seen them," she thought. The road now hardly showed in the thick dusk. Ruth stumbled often, and began to be both hungry and thirsty. She wished she could stop and rest; but the thought of Winifred sitting alone under the big oak tree made her resolve not to stop until she reached home.

At last she could see an open space ahead, and the dark line of the river; and at the same moment she heard the sound of trotting feet on the road behind her and a little gray figure ran swiftly by.

"That was Fluff! I know it was Fluff," she exclaimed, and called loudly after the pony. But Fluff did not stop; he knew he was headed for home, and it was much easier to run along free and unharnessed than to pull a cart containing two little girls.

Ruth now hardly knew what to do. Perhaps Winifred might be coming closely behind the pony.

"Perhaps I ought to wait and see if she is coming," thought Ruth, puzzled and uncertain as to the right course to take. Before she could decide she saw the gleam of a lantern, and heard the wheels of a carriage coming rapidly over the road, and without a moment's hesitation she called out: "Stop! Please stop!" and heard a familiar voice respond:

"It's Ruth. It's Ruth." And the light of the lantern showed Gilbert and his mother in Ned Ferris's pony-cart.

In a moment they were standing in the road beside her, and Ruth was telling the story of the woodland road, and of Winifred waiting beside the pony-cart under a big oak tree.

"And Fluff just ran by, headed for home," she concluded.

"I thought it was Fluff who raced past us. I was sure it was he," said Gilbert.

They were now puzzled what course to take. To leave Winifred alone so far from any human habitation was not to be thought of; neither did Mrs. Merrill wish Ruth to go on toward home without some one with her.

"Gilbert, you must go home with Ruth, and I will drive on after Winifred," she decided. Mrs. Pennell will be sadly troubled when Fluff comes running home and she has no news of her little girl. Go as quickly as you can."

Gilbert agreed; but he felt a little defrauded as he and Ruth turned toward home. He would have enjoyed going up that dark hillside road, where it seemed to him some interesting adventure might befall a traveler.

Mrs. Merrill, with the lantern fastened to the front of the cart, drove rapidly up the hill, trying to pierce the dusky shadows of the roadside. Now and then she called Winifred's name, and listened intently for some response, but none came.

At last the light from the lantern showed the pony-carriage in the shadow of the big oak tree, and in a moment Mrs. Merrill was on the ground beside it. But Winifred was not to be seen. "Winifred!" she called over and over, but there was no reply.

CHAPTER XIII

HOME AGAIN

WINIFRED awakened suddenly. For a moment she looked about with startled eyes.

"Winifred! Winifred!"

"That is Mother calling," she exclaimed aloud, springing to her feet, and resting one hand against the smooth trunk of the pine tree. For a moment she was too surprised and sleepy to respond to the call; then she called back, "Mother! I'm in the woods!" at the same time moving slowly around to the other side of the big tree.

"Oh! There's a light! And there's the road! And there is Mother!" and stumbling and running Winifred appeared in the road only a short distance from the flickering light of the lantern.

"Mother! Mother! Did you come all alone?" called Winifred, as her mother held her close as if, thought the little girl, "I had been away a long time."

"I thought I was way in the deep woods, and I was close to the road all the time. But Fluff is lost," she explained, as her mother led her toward the cart.

"No, dear; Fluff passed us on our way home, and will probably be safe in his stall long before we get back," replied Mrs. Merrill, and as they drove through the darkness she told her little daughter of how troubled she and Mrs. Pennell had been as the afternoon passed and Winifred and Ruth failed to return; of Gilbert borrowing Ned's pony, of meeting Ruth, "and I have been here an hour, calling and calling," she concluded.

"How sound asleep I must have been not to hear you," said Winifred happily, snuggling closer to her mother's side.

"After Fluff ran off I began to be frightened," she continued. "I thought of catamounts and bears; and then I thought of my sampler."

"Your sampler?" repeated Mrs. Merrill, not understanding just what Winifred meant.

"Yes, Mother dear! Don't you remember the words you traced on it? 'There shall no evil befall thee. For he shall give his angels charge over thee, to keep thee in all thy ways,'" repeated the little girl. "I kept saying it over and over and I was not afraid."

For a moment Mrs. Merrill did not reply. She stooped and kissed her little daughter, and then said: "That was right, dear child."

It was nearly midnight when Mrs. Merrill and Winifred reached home, and Gilbert lifted a very sleepy little girl from the pony-cart. "Mrs. Pennell and Ruth are here," he said, "and she has some hot broth ready."

Gilbert looked after Ned's pony before following his mother and sister into the house. Mrs. Pennell had already prepared his supper and he had eaten it with Ruth on reaching home after their long walk; but that seemed a long time ago, and he was quite ready to sit down at the candle-lit table and join the others. The hot broth, toast and damson preserves were very welcome to Winifred and her mother. The little group around the table were all too tired to talk much, but they smiled happily at one another, rejoicing that they were all safe and at home.

It was decided that Mrs. Pennell and Ruth should stay the remainder of the night with the Merrills.

"Hero will take care of our house," Ruth said confidently, as she and her mother entered the pleasant chamber where they were to sleep.

"Mother, you never scold me, do you?" she said, just as Mrs. Pennell extinguished the candle, and smiled happily to herself at her mother's little laugh.

"Why, Ruthie dear! I should hope not. You know 'scold' is an ugly word. There is nothing about it that is fair. It means to 'find fault,' which is never quite fair; do you think it is?" and Ruth agreed that "scold" had an ugly sound.

"We didn't mean to stay away and to worry you," said Ruth.

"Of course you didn't, dear child. Go to sleep," replied her mother, who was thinking to herself that no other little girl was as dear and good as her own little daughter. And, strange as it may seem, Mrs. Merrill was thinking that very same thing about Winifred.

How much there was for the two little friends to talk about the next day! Gilbert and Fluff had started off at an early hour to bring home the pony-cart, and early in the afternoon Betty Hastings came to see Ruth. She knew nothing about the adventure of the day before, and listened eagerly to Ruth and Winifred as they told of the lonely road, the coming of darkness, and of the deer and fawn that Ruth had seen.

The two younger girls looked at Betty admiringly as they all sat together in Mrs. Pennell's front room. Betty's smooth brown curls under her pretty white straw hat, her shining brown eyes and pleasant smile, and the pretty dress of blue and white plaid, made her well worth their approving glances. Both Ruth and Winifred wondered to themselves why it was that Betty's hands were always clean, her hair smooth, and her dress always neat and in order. They decided, as they had often done before, that it was because Betty was so nearly grown up, nearly thirteen. They were quite sure that being tidy and careful was a gift that came with years.

Ruth always liked to have Betty come to see her.

"It's just like really being grown up when Betty comes," she had explained to her mother, "because we always sit in the front room, and never play dolls." So this afternoon when Mrs. Pennell brought in a tray with the little silver pitcher and sugar bowl, the lustre teapot, and the treasured Canton cups and saucers, together with a plate of round frosted cakes, and Ruth had the pleasure of giving Betty and Winifred a cup of "real tea" she felt herself the most fortunate little girl in Philadelphia.

" 'Tis not a taxed tea," Mrs. Pennell declared smilingly; for Americans had refused to receive any tea on which the Government of Great Britain demanded an unlawful tax.

"I came to ask you and Winifred to a May party," said Betty, when she was ready to start for home. "My mother says I may invite a dozen girls to go Maying to some pleasant place on the river, where we can gather flowers, put up a May-pole, and have a picnic lunch. Mother will get some one to drive us all out in a big wagon."

Both Ruth and Winifred were delighted at the invitation, and thanked Betty. May-day was nearly two weeks distant, but they were glad to have so pleasant an invitation. And the front door had hardly closed behind their visitor when Ruth exclaimed:

"We must begin on that table right away, Winifred, so that it will surely be finished by May-day. I have just remembered that May first is Betty's birthday! Her mother always has a party for her."

"So it is!" responded Winifred, as she followed Ruth toward the shed.

There was a piece of chalk in the drawer of the work-bench, and Ruth, laying the square of smooth dark wood on the top of a barrel, began to mark a large heart, while Winifred stood beside her watching admiringly.

"There!" Ruth exclaimed, as her rather uneven chalk line came to an end. "I guess that is enough to go by. We can make the edges smooth with some of the tools."

Winifred agreed promptly. "I'll make the legs," she volunteered.

"Be sure and have them all the same length," advised Ruth. "You can take this chalk and mark the places where to saw;" and in a few moments Winifred with a small sharp saw was endeavoring to cut through the strips of hard wood selected for table legs, while Ruth with a sharp knife tried in vain to make some impression on the square of mahogany. Snap! went the slender knife-blade!

"Oh, Winifred! quick! I've cut off my thumb!" screamed Ruth, as she raced past the horrified Winifred and ran into the kitchen calling: "Mother! Mother!"

In a moment her mother was beside her; the injured thumb was bathed and bandaged, and Ruth was explaining, with Winifred's help, how the accident occurred. It was really a deep cut, and it was no wonder that the little girl had been frightened.

Mrs. Pennell went to the shed with the little girls, and looked with troubled eyes at the cherished pieces of polished wood, and the fine tools scattered about the floor.

"We must put all these tools carefully back in the chest, and the wood on the shelf just as your father left it. Winifred will help me, for you must not use your hand, Ruth," she said.

"But, Mother, we want to make a heart-shaped table for a birthday present for Betty," Ruth explained. "Mayn't we use Father's tools?"

"No, my dear. It would have been a very serious thing if you had spoiled any of his saws or planes. And those strips and squares of wood are valuable. Besides that you and Winifred are not accustomed to the use of tools; and you might really have cut off your thumb instead of only cutting it," said Mrs. Pennell. "I am to blame that I did not tell you how much your dear father valued these tools and wood."

"Oh, Mother! You are never to blame. I ought to have asked you," Ruth declared.

"Well, my dear, I really think it would have been wiser. But now we must think of something else as a present for Betty. With that hurt thumb, Ruth, I am afraid you cannot make her anything," responded her mother, leading the way to the seat under the maple tree.

"Now, let us all try and think of something that Betty would like for a birthday gift," she continued, as they all sat down. Hero came bounding across the yard, and took his usual place at Ruth's feet.

"I know! I know exactly what Betty would like," declared Ruth, "and I am sure I could help make it. Candy! She loves candy. Can I not use some of your sugar, Mother, to make some heart-shaped sweets?" For Ruth had some tiny heart-shaped molds of tin, into which hot candy mixture could be turned, and that when cool came out in perfect shapes.

"That will be better than a table," said Winifred eagerly, "and I know my mother will give me some sugar for such a purpose. And, Ruth! we can make a heart-shaped box of paper to put it in."

Mrs. Pennell listened smilingly as the two little girls made their plan for their friend's birthday gift. She promised to give them a portion of her scanty store of sugar.

"You will not need to make it for a week to come; and Ruth's thumb will be well by that time. You may have the kitchen to yourselves on the last day of April," she said.

Ruth quite forgot the ugly cut in her excitement over the proposed candy-making.

"I am glad May is only ten days away," she said. "Just think of all that is going to happen next month! Betty's birthday picnic, and my visit to Aunt Deborah! And perhaps even more than that. Perhaps I shall see Lafayette! And perhaps the English will leave Philadelphia."

Both her mother and Winifred laughed at Ruth's eager prophecy.

CHAPTER XIV

THE CANDY DISAPPEARS

GILBERT and Winifred often talked to Ruth of their soldier brother, Vinal; and she never tired of hearing the story of a midnight visit he had made during the previous winter.

He had arrived home late one afternoon, coming up the street as if there were not an English soldier in the city, and had stayed the night in his own home, departing early the next morning for Valley Forge. It was just such an adventure as the children admired, and would have well liked to have had some part in.

Gilbert had reluctantly given up the plan of changing his name to Lafayette. No one seemed to remember his wish, and after a few weeks he no longer reminded Ruth or Winifred.

As the time of Ruth's visit to Barren Hill drew near she made many pleasant plans of all she would see and do while at Aunt Deborah's square stone house, and recalled all that her aunt had told her of the bee-hives in a sunny corner of the garden, the flocks of chickens, the many birds that nested safely in the orchard trees, and the big attic that would be such a fine play-house on stormy days. But most of all Ruth thought of the fact that Barren Hill was only ten miles distant from Valley Forge, and that there might be some way in which she could see her father.

"I wish I could find out that the English were going to leave Philadelphia, and then I would have good news for Father," she thought. "Or if I could carry a fine present for Father to give Lafayette." But there seemed little prospect that a little girl like Ruth could be the bearer of good news to the troops at Valley Forge, or of a present to the gallant young Frenchman.

Ruth's thumb healed in a few days, so that she could help her mother in the garden, and do her usual work about the house. Every morning, direct- ly after breakfast, was the lesson hour, when Mrs. Pennell and Ruth would sit down in the dining-room and, as Ruth had described it to Aunt Deborah, "Tell stories."

There were "history" stories, and these Ruth liked best of all. One was the story of the first Quaker emi- grants who came to Philadelphia in three small ships, bringing a friendly letter from the good-natured King Charles to the Delaware Indians. She liked to hear how these people sailed safely across the Atlantic and came up the Delaware, and first found shelter in caves along the river's bank, and then built themselves log cabins, and big strong houses.

Then there were stories of the stars, by which sailors steered their course at sea, and there were stories of birds and beasts, and a very amusing game in which a small girl from Japan and another from China, and a little black girl from Africa, each recited the way children were taught in those countries.

Mrs. Pennell did not always tell the stories, no, indeed! Often Ruth would be asked to tell the story of William Penn, or perhaps to draw a little picture of certain constellations. And always there was the adding of apples, the dividing of apples into four parts and eight parts, which Mrs. Pennell called "Fractions." And after this pleasant hour there were the neat stitches to be set in apron, dress, or handkerchief.

Nearly every child had regular tasks; they were taught to use their hands as well as their eyes and thoughts, and Ruth was very proud that she could hemstitch nicely, and "set the heel" of a stocking, and finish off its toe.

After Vinal brought the letter from Ruth's father Mrs. Pennell seemed more cheerful, and often said that she was sure it would not be many months before Philadelphia would be rid of the enemy.

Ruth and Winifred counted the days until the last day of April, when they were to make the candy as a present for Betty. The pretty heart-shaped box that was to hold it was already finished. Mrs. Pennell had helped them make it. She had carefully shaped it from paste-board, and then, with a flour paste, the little girls had covered it carefully with some pretty bits of wall-paper. The cover had three tiny hearts cut from gilt paper, and Ruth and Winifred were both sure that Betty would be much pleased by their gift, especially when she opened it and found it full of sweets.

Ruth had just finished her lesson hour on the morning of the day before the May-day picnic, when Winifred appeared. She brought a package of sugar that her mother had given her as her share for the candy, and the two little girls ran to the kitchen, which they were to have quite to themselves for their candy-making.

The family cooking was done over the bed of coals in the fireplace, and Ruth brought out a saucepan, a big spoon, and some sugar from the pantry, and talking happily of the pleasures of the coming day the two little friends measured their sugar and set the saucepan over the coals, while Ruth, spoon in hand, watched it carefully, while Winifred stood close by ready to help.

It was a great event to be permitted to make candy, and both Winifred and Ruth decided that it would be a much more acceptable present than a table.

In a short time the melted sugar, flavored with rose leaves, was ready to be turned into the tiny heart-shaped molds, and set to cool on the window ledge.

"Let's go out in the garden," suggested Ruth. "If we stay in here we shall keep looking at the candy to see if it is ready to turn out, and it will seem forever." So they went out to the seat under the maple tree, played with Hero, talked about the May party and the time, now near at hand, when Ruth would go to visit Aunt Deborah, and nearly an hour passed before they returned to the kitchen.

"Why, where are the molds?" exclaimed Ruth. "Where is the candy?" demanded Winifred, and they looked at the vacant window-sill where they had left the sweets to cool.

"Mother must have put them in the pantry," said Ruth.

"Of course," Winifred agreed, and the little girls exchanged a smile of relief as they both turned toward the pantry.

But the candy was not there.

"I'll run and ask her where she put it," said Ruth, and hurried off to find her mother who was busy in one of the upper rooms.

"But I have not been down-stairs, dear child," Mrs. Pennell replied. "You do not suppose the molds have fallen out of the window?" she asked, and without stopping to answer Ruth ran back to the kitchen, and leaned out of the window, but there was no candy to be seen.

"Oh, Ruth! The box is gone, too! Some one must have come in and taken it!" said Winifred; and, sure enough, the pretty box had disappeared from the table as well as the molds from the window. Both the little girls were ready to cry with disappointment.

They knew that each of the other guests would bring Betty a present, and they knew also that their mothers could not spare any more sugar for candy. Besides this the pretty box was gone, and they had no more bits of paper to make another.

"I shan't go to the party," Ruth declared. "And who could have been mean enough to take the candy?"

Mrs. Pennell was nearly as troubled as Ruth and Winnie. It was evident that some one must have entered the house by the front door, taken the candy, and made off while the girls were in the garden. She feared that other things must have been taken, but a careful search proved that nothing else was missing.

Winifred agreed with Ruth that they did not wish to go to the party without a present for Betty. "And now it is too late to even think of anything," she said as she started for home, leaving Ruth puzzled and unhappy, and wondering to herself if perhaps some ill-natured fairies had not made off with the sweets. The more Ruth thought of this the more convinced she was that it was what had happened. She remembered hearing queer little noises at her window that morning that she had thought were made by the birds nesting in the hawthorn. Now she said to herself that it must have been fairies coming into the house. "And because I did not make them welcome they have taken the candy," she decided, remembering a fairy tale that Mrs. Merrill had once told the two girls in which children had always welcomed fairies who came tapping at the windows of a spring morning, by singing:

> "Welcome, fairies good and kind;
> Come in, come in, and welcome find."

In the story the fairies had brought wonderful gifts, but if they had not been welcomed they would have taken the children's dearest possessions, which could only be recovered by walking around the garden just before sunrise and bowing low three times to the lilac, three times to a robin, and three times with your eyes shut tight, repeating each time:

> "Fairies, fairies, here I bow.
> Will you kindly pardon now
> That I did not hear or see
> When you came to visit me?"

Ruth was glad that she could remember it.

"I'll get up before sunrise to-morrow morning and do exactly as the little girl did in the story when the fairies brought back her silver heart, and then probably when I open my eyes there will be the box and the candy," thought Ruth.

"Why, of course, it was because the box and the candies were heart-shaped," she decided; "that's another reason I'm sure it was fairies. It will be splendid if I can get them back. I won't tell Winifred until after breakfast to-morrow. Won't she be surprised?"

Mrs. Pennell wondered a little that Ruth was in such good spirits the rest of the day, after the disappearance of the candy, and that she was so ready to go to bed at an hour earlier than the usual time.

CHAPTER XV

A FAIRY STORY

WHEN Gilbert took the pan of candy-molds from the open window of Mrs. Pennell's kitchen, and, reaching in captured the heart-shaped box from the table, his only intention was to keep them just long enough to puzzle Ruth and Winifred and then return them. When the girls came back to the kitchen he had run into the shed, and set box and pan in the open drawer of the work-bench and closed it quickly, and had then gone home to attend to some garden work, meaning to come back in an hour at the longest; but his mother had sent him on an errand, and it was noon before Gilbert remembered the candy; and then Winifred was telling the story of its disappearance:

"You wouldn't think any one would be so mean as to take our candy," she concluded, and Gilbert felt his face flush uncomfortably, and realized that it was going to be very difficult to explain what he had intended for a joke to Ruth and Winifred. In some way he must get that candy and box back to the place from which he had taken it, or else tell the girls what he had done; and this last alternative would be unpleasant. All that afternoon he was on the alert for a chance to slip into the Pennells' garden, enter the shed and rescue the hidden sweets; but the day was warm and pleasant, and Ruth and Winifred with their dolls and Hero were out-of-doors playing about in the shade of the maple tree until it was too late for Gilbert to carry out his plan; so that he was as uneasy and troubled as Ruth or Winifred over the missing candy, and not until evening could he think of any way to recover it.

He was just closing the stable for the night when he noticed the shallow basket of woven grass and twigs which Winifred had made on the eventful afternoon's journey along the river road. The violets and wild honeysuckle were now only dried up stems; but the basket looked serviceable and attractive. Gilbert smiled as he picked it up. He knew now exactly what he would do: he would get up very early the next morning, gather daffodils and iris and then take the basket to Mrs. Pennell's shed,—take the candy from the molds, fill the box, and setting the box in Winifred's grass basket cover it with flowers; then he would hang it to the knocker of the Pennells' front door.

"The girls will think the fairies did it for a May-day surprise," he chuckled to himself, remembering that Winifred could never quite decide about fairies: if there really were such wonderful little people or not.

So Gilbert was up before sunrise the next morning, and with a friendly word to Hero, found it an easy matter to enter the shed quietly and take the candy and box from the bench drawer. In a few moments he had filled the box skilfully without breaking one of the tiny hearts, set it in the basket and covered it with the spring blossoms. He was just about to leave the shed when he heard a voice, and peering out saw Ruth bowing to the lilac tree and saying in a low voice:

"Fairies, fairies, here I bow.
Will you kindly pardon now
That I did not hear or see
When you came to visit me?"

"Jiminy! It's that old fairy story Mother tells; and Ruth believes it," thought Gilbert, as he watched Ruth bowing low to a startled robin, which flew up to a higher branch in the hawthorn tree. She was so much absorbed in what she was doing that she did not hear the stealthy step behind her on the soft grass as Gilbert swiftly set down the mold pan and the basket, and flew back to the shop. He had just reached its shelter when Ruth turned to go back to the house and saw the basket.

She looked at it for a moment as if she could hardly believe her eyes; and as she stooped to pick it up Ruth fully expected that basket, pan and tin molds would all vanish from sight. But no! They were real;

and, quite as Ruth expected, the box, filled with candy hearts, was under the flowers.

"Oh! what will Winifred say?" she whispered to herself. And then she bowed to the lilac tree and to the robin, and said, "Thank you, kind fairies. I will always know now that you are true and kind," and then Ruth ran into the house to wake up her mother and tell her this wonderful story, and show her the basket in proof of the fairies' visit.

Gilbert hurried home. He was delighted with the success of his plan, but a little troubled that Ruth should believe so implicitly that fairies had first taken and then returned the candy.

Mrs. Pennell listened to Ruth's story and looked at the basket with as much wonder and surprise as even Ruth could expect. Although she did not deny that fairies had a hand in the return of the candy, she endeavored to explain to herself just how it could have occurred. But she remembered how much happiness she herself had had as a small girl in believing in good fairies, and was quite willing that her own little daughter should have the same pleasure.

The Merrills were just sitting down to an early breakfast when Ruth came over to tell Winifred that the candy had been found, but she did not tell all the story, for she knew Gilbert laughed at fairies.

"I'll tell you all about it on the way to Betty's," she said, for it had been arranged that Betty's guests should all meet at her house, where the wagons would be in readiness to take them to a favorite picnic ground, a green sloping field on the banks of the Schuylkill River, where there were groups of wide-spreading elms and where many spring flowers grew.

Winifred was so eager to hear about the return of the candy that she could hardly wait to finish her breakfast. Ruth had not lingered after telling the great news, but had run home to make ready for the picnic.

Gilbert continued to feel uneasy about his part in the fairy story, and after Ruth and Winifred had started for the May party he followed his mother into the garden and offered to help her transplant the young seedlings.

"Mother, do you think there is any harm in believing in fairies?" he asked, and before his mother could reply Gilbert was telling her the story.

"Ruth seemed more pleased about the fairies than she did to get the candy back," he concluded, "and I don't think there is any harm in fairies, do you?"

"Why, no, Gilbert! I am always hoping that they really are true," replied his mother smilingly.

"Oh, Mother! You are as bad as Ruth," laughed Gilbert; "but do you think I ought to tell Ruth that I hid the candy, and then brought it back?"

"No, not at present. Some time in the future you can tell Ruth about it, if you wish, but I think it would be too bad to spoil her pleasure to-day. But perhaps you had better ask Mrs. Pennell, and then do whatever she thinks best," replied his mother.

The thought of telling Mrs. Pennell of his mischievous act made Gilbert rather uncomfortable, but he responded promptly:

"All right, Mother. I'll go now," and ran toward the house to wash his hands before presenting himself at Mrs. Pennell's door.

"So that was it. I could not imagine how it happened," said Mrs. Pennell when Gilbert had told of hiding the candy, and of meaning to return it as a May basket. She agreed with Mrs. Merrill that Ruth could be told the facts later on, and did not seem to feel that Gilbert's joke had been anything but natural and harmless, so Gilbert returned home with an untroubled mind.

Betty had asked her little guests to be at her house at half-past ten o'clock, and when Ruth and Winifred came down the street they saw a big wagon with two big brown horses standing in front of Betty's house; just behind the big wagon was a smaller one which Dinah was helping to load with baskets and packages.

"That's the lunch wagon," said Winifred. "Oh, Ruth! I'm sure we are going to have a beautiful time. What do you suppose Betty will say when you tell her about the fairies?"

"I don't know. But probably she will think she is lucky to have a basket made by fairies," responded Ruth, who did not know the story of the basket that she carried so carefully.

"I made that basket. Truly I did, Ruth," Winifred declared eagerly.

Ruth's smile vanished. She stood still and looked at Winifred accusingly.

"Then I suppose there weren't any fairies at all? If you made the basket you probably put the candy in it and set it in my garden for me to find. And you let me tell you all about bowing to the lilac tree, and never said a word," exclaimed Ruth; "and I suppose you have been laughing at me all the time," she concluded, a little choke coming in her throat at the thought that her best friend, as well as the fairies, had failed her.

Before Winifred could say a word Ruth ran ahead as fast as she could go. Betty was on the steps, and a number of the girls who were going on the picnic were with her. She greeted Ruth warmly, and when Ruth explained that the basket was from Winifred and herself Betty was greatly pleased. She was looking at the basket and box admiringly when Winnie appeared.

"Did Ruth tell you that is a fairy present?" she asked eagerly, and at the little chorus of laughter and questions, Winifred went on and told the story just as Ruth had told it to her, while Ruth stood by looking rather sulky and unhappy. The moment Winifred finished Ruth stepped forward and said:

"That's a good story, but it isn't true. About the fairies, I mean. Not one word of it. And Winifred knows it isn't."

CHAPTER XVI

BETTY AND ANNETTE

THE girls' laughter ceased, and they looked at Ruth a little questioningly as if expecting that she would explain. But it was Betty who, slipping her arm around Winifred, said pleasantly: "Well, we are all obliged to Winnie for telling us such a beautiful story. And I am sure it is just what the fairies would do if they happened to think of it."

Winifred looked up at the older girl gratefully, but she felt very unhappy. She could not understand why Ruth, her very best friend, should have turned against her, and denied the story.

Ruth stood, sulky and silent, and a little ashamed, as the other guests arrived; and when Betty declared that it was time to start and led the way toward the big wagon, Ruth walked alone and was the last one of Betty's guests to climb up to her seat.

There were ten little girls in the party, and Black Jason, Dinah's husband, was to drive the team. Mrs. Hastings sat on the back seat between Betty and Ruth; the small wagon with the good things for the birthday luncheon followed close behind, driven by a friend of Jason's.

The other girls laughed and talked merrily as the big horses trotted briskly through the streets leading to the river. But Ruth was silent, except when Mrs. Hastings spoke to her; then she answered as pleasantly as possible, but she had no pleasure in the ride. Now and then they passed groups of English soldiers; and as they turned into the river road several red-coated officers on horseback rode past them.

"We wish you a happy May, young ladies," called one of the officers, bowing very low as he rode past the wagon filled with happy girls.

There was no response to his polite salutation; for even the children of the historic city resented the presence of the English soldiery.

"Mother, sing your May-day song," suggested Betty.

But Mrs. Hastings shook her head laughingly.

"I must save that for our dance round the May-pole," she replied, "and we shall soon be at the picnic field now."

The field was very near the place where Ruth and Winifred had turned into the hill road, and the May party reached it after not more than an hour's ride. Black Jason drove through the field toward the river bank, and stopped under a group of tall elms. In a few moments the girls were scattered about searching for flowers. Black Jason and his friend unloaded the lunch wagon, and then Mrs. Hastings called the girls to decide on the best place to erect the May-pole, a fine birch tree that Black Jason was now chopping down.

"There are so many good places!" exclaimed Betty, looking about the smooth field. "I think this is the best," she decided finally, as, with her guests beside her, she stopped near the edge of a wood.

It was just the place for a May-pole, the other girls declared, as they looked about; and Black Jason and his friend set up the tall birch tree, whose green branches were more beautiful than any decoration that the girls could have imagined. While Mrs. Hastings and Betty spread the lunch in the shade of the woods, the other girls gathered flowers and wove garlands for each other, and talked happily together. Ruth found herself seated beside Annette Tennant, a girl about Betty's age.

"I will give you my wreath, and you can give me yours," said the older girl. "You are rather young to be asked to this party," she continued, looking at Ruth.

"I am nearly eleven," replied Ruth. "Winifred Merrill isn't any older than that."

"I noticed there were two little girls," rejoined Annette condescendingly. "You mustn't mind if most of us are older. I always like children," went on

Annette, who was even taller than Betty Hastings, and whose yellow hair was braided neatly and wound around her head.

Ruth made no reply. She was feeling a little ashamed that she had declared Winifred's story to be untrue. Even if Winnie had set the basket in the garden and let her go about bowing to trees and birds Ruth felt that she herself had been rude and unkind.

"What made that other child tell all that rigmarole about fairies?" questioned Annette. "I was glad when you spoke up and said that it was not true. Of course we older girls knew she was making it up."

Suddenly Ruth became perfectly sure that Winifred had had nothing to do with the discovery of the candy, and that Winifred had really believed the fairies had brought it back, using her basket for the purpose.

"Winifred didn't make it up," declared Ruth. "It was exactly as she told it. The fairies did take away the candy, and bring it back."

Annette stopped weaving the vines and flowers, and jumped up.

"Well, you are a very funny child. You tell us all that Winifred Merrill made up a story, and now you tell me that it was true," she exclaimed scornfully. "You need not give me your garland; I don't want it, or anything to do with you," and before Ruth could say a word in reply Annette had joined a group of the older girls, and was evidently telling them her opinion of Ruth Pennell.

Ruth looked down through a blur of tears at the wreath she was making. She could hardly see the flowers in her lap.

"I wish I had stayed at home. I hate grown-up girls," she thought bitterly, wishing herself in her own garden with Hero and Cecilia for playmates.

The sound of Betty's voice calling to her guests that luncheon was ready made Ruth look up. She saw the other girls walking toward the shade of the tall elms where Mrs. Hastings stood waiting for them.

Winifred was evidently in high favor; Annette walked on one side and Mary Pierce on the other, each with an arm about the pleased but somewhat embarrassed Winifred.

"Ruth! Ruthie Pennell! We are all waiting for you," called Betty, and Ruth followed the others.

It was evident at once that none of the girls meant to sit beside Ruth if it could be avoided. Annette had declared that she believed Ruth to be a mischief-maker, and untruthful, and that it was the duty of the older girls to "teach her a lesson."

"We must let the child realize that older girls don't approve of such things," Annette had said, and the others agreed that the best way to express their disapproval was to leave Ruth to herself as much as possible.

Winifred was now more puzzled than ever. When Annette had repeated Ruth's declaration that Winifred's story was true, that fairies had returned the candy, she did not know what to think.

"I'm sure Ruthie was only fooling," Winifred declared bravely. "I mean when she said that I made up the story about the candy. Because it was just what she told me."

"Then the child must be taught that we don't like such fooling," responded Annette, with what she felt was a very grown-up and impressive manner.

"Sit here, Ruth," said Betty, wondering at the manner of the older girls, "and, Winifred, come and sit beside her."

Winifred was quite ready to change her seat as Betty suggested, but Annette's hand clasped her arm, and it was Annette who answered: "Winnie would rather sit here, beside me.

"All right," responded Betty. "Then I'll have Ruthie for my helper. I can always depend on you, Ruth, can't I?" she added, smiling at her young friend.

"Always," whispered Ruth, gratefully; and it was she who helped Betty serve the other girls with the excellent cold chicken, and bread, and butter, the jelly-filled tarts, and squares of molasses gingerbread, so that Annette's proposed "lesson" bid fair to be defeated.

"What's the matter, Ruthie?" Betty found a chance to whisper, as they sat down together a little way from the larger group.

Ruth told the story eagerly. "I don't know why I thought Winnie had put the basket there, or why I was so horrid as to say that she told a story," confessed the unhappy little girl. "Do you suppose it really was the fairies, Betty?"

Betty looked rather sober for a minute. She was thinking to herself that her May-day party bid fair to be a failure unless her guests could realize that Ruth had only made a mistake for which she was sorry. She blamed Annette more than she did Ruth, feeling sure that Winifred and Ruth would have come to a friendly understanding if Annette had not interfered.

"I have a plan, Ruthie, that perhaps will make it all right. Will you do just what I tell you?"

"Yes, indeed I will," responded Ruth gratefully.

Mrs. Hastings had left the girls to themselves and gone over to the May-pole.

"Come here, Winifred," called Betty, and this time Annette made no objection, and in a moment

Winifred was sitting beside Ruth, and both the little girls were thinking that Betty was much nicer than any other "grown-up" girl in the party.

"Ruth Pennell is going to tell us a story," announced Betty. "She doesn't know if it really is true or not. For a little while she thought her best friend had taken the part of a fairy, but afterward she was sure she had not. Now, Ruth," and Betty turned smilingly toward her little friend, "stand up and tell us all about it; about the making of my candy, how it disappeared, and what you did to recover it. Then, when you have finished, we will take a vote and see how many of us believe in fairies."

For a moment Ruth hesitated, but Winifred's friendly smile encouraged her and she stood up. She did not look at the group of girls sitting about under the trees; she looked straight over their heads at the river, and began to speak, beginning her story with the discovery that the candy had disappeared. She spoke clearly, and when she finished by saying that she was sorry that she had been rude to Winifred, because she and Winifred both rather believed in fairies, there was a little murmur of approval.

"Now, girls, all those who believe in fairies stand up," said Betty, jumping to her feet, and reaching out a hand to the girls beside her, and at the same time beginning to sing:

" 'Here are fields of smiling flowers—
　Come and seek May in her bowers.
　　Catch young May.
　　Make her stay;
　Dance around her bright and gay.'"

Nearly all the girls knew the song and joined in singing, as hand in hand they ran across the smooth grass toward the May-pole, where Mrs. Hastings stood waiting for them. And now Ruth was her happy, smiling self again, and Annette was no longer eager to teach "lessons" to the younger girls. Annette and Ruth were both conscious, however, that Betty, with her frank kindness, had smoothed out their mistakes.

CHAPTER XVII

QUEEN BETTY

THE girls had exchanged their wreaths of flowers as they sat down to luncheon, all excepting Ruth and Annette, who wore the ones they had made themselves, and they now made a very attractive picture as they all formed a ring around the May-pole, singing an old song that their mothers had sung when they too were little girls; a May-pole song that had been sung in England for hundreds of years.

> " 'Round the May-pole, trit, trit, trot.
> See what a garland we have got:
> Fine and gay,
> Trip away.
> Happy is our New May Day.' "

"Now for choosing the May Queen!" said Mary Pierce, and a little chorus of "Betty Hastings! Betty Hastings!" was the response, and Betty curtsied very low, and thanked her guests. For "Maids of Honor" she chose Ruth and Winifred, whose duties were to walk one on each side of the May Queen on her way to her throne, and then kneel beside her until she bade them rise.

"THE FIRST OF MAY IS GARLAND DAY"

While the girls had been at luncheon and dancing around the May-pole Black Jason and his friend had been busily at work behind some thick growing trees near the river.

"All ready, Missie!" he announced, as, hat in hand, and bowing low, he came smilingly toward the "Queen of the May."

A little procession formed to follow Jason, who led the way through a woodland path to a clearing that opened toward the river. In this clearing stood a big rustic chair, Betty"s "throne."

Ruth and Winifred handed the Queen to her seat with great ceremony, and then one after another the girls approached the throne, curtsying low and laying their garlands at Betty's feet. Now they joined hands in a little circle, and danced around the throne, singing:

> " 'The First of May is garland day,
>   And every child should dance and play.
>   Curl your locks as I do mine,
>   And wear your summer gown so fine.'"

The Queen of the May asks any favor she pleases from the throne, but as soon as she leaves the throne her power ceases; so now the group of laughing girls stood waiting to hear what the Queen would ask:

> "A wreath and a staff
>   And a cup to quaff,"

demanded Betty smilingly, and away raced her loyal subjects to fulfil the royal demand.

It was Annette who brought the wreath of violets; Mary Pierce came with a curving branch that Jason had cut from a maple tree and trimmed into a staff, while Caroline Fraser brought a cup of cool water from the spring under the willow tree.

"We must soon be thinking of home," Mrs. Hastings reminded them, as the girls, now flushed and a little tired, seated themselves about the throne, from which Betty had descended.

"You have not sung your May-day song, Mother!" Betty reminded her, and the girls now gathered about Mrs. Hastings, repeating Betty's request.

"But it isn't really 'my' song; it is an old English May song," Mrs. Hastings said.

> "'Spring is coming, Spring is coming,
>   Flowers are coming too;
>   Pansies, lilies, daffodilies,
>   Now are coming through.
>
> "'Spring is coming, Spring is coming,
>   All around is fair;
>   Shimmer and quiver on the river
>   Joy is everywhere.'"

As she finished singing Mrs. Hastings curtsied to the happy group, and said:

"I wish you a happy May."

When Black Jason drove the brown horses into the field, and the girls took their seats in the wagon, they all declared it was the best May-day party they had ever known, and they all thought Betty Hastings was the most fortunate of girls that her birthday came on the first day of May.

"How would you and Winifred like to sit with Jason on the front seat, Ruth?" asked Mrs. Hastings, and the two little friends smiled at each other, and replied that they would like it very much, and so were lifted to the high seat beside the good-natured Jason.

"I almost spoiled everything," Ruth whispered to Winifred, "but Betty made it come out all right. I like Betty."

"So do I," responded Winifred, and they smiled at each other again, both quite sure that they would never again come so near to a quarrel as they had that May-day.

As they drove past a square stone house whose gardens sloped down to the river, Black Jason pointed toward it with his whip and said: "Dat de house where Capt'n Delancy live, an' he an' de oder fine English soldiers are gettin' up a great party, a kind of show like."

The girls looked well at the house from which Betty had so skilfully made her escape on the night following Gilbert's play.

"Are they going to have the party in that house, Jason?" asked Ruth.

"Landy! No, Missie. It's to be out to Master Wharton's fine place in Southwark. Folks do say as General Sir Willum Howe be gwine to leave dis place. They certain do say so," and Jason chuckled with satisfaction at the thought.

"Then will General Washington and Lafayette come here, Jason?" questioned Ruth eagerly.

"I dunno, Missie. But I reckon de English gwine to have a mighty fine party. Dere gwine to have bands o' music in boats on de river. Yas'm," and Jason chuckled at the thought of all the great preparations that had already begun for the most splendid pageant that America had seen, and about which the people of Philadelphia were wondering, for the English officers were making elaborate plans.

"I wish I could drive two horses," said Ruth, looking a little longingly at the reins and whip that Jason so skilfully held in one hand.

"Landy, Missie! Yo' jes' take hold de reins like dis," responded Jason, at the same moment clasping Ruth's hands over the leather reins. "Now hole 'em stiddy."

Ruth obeyed Jason's instructions to "look straight ahead, an' hole 'em up stiddy," and it was the happiest part of all that happy May-day to be driving Jason's brown horses, with the other girls singing and laughing on the seats behind her. But as they turned from the river road into the town Jason again took the reins. The girls were now carried each to her own home, so Winifred and Ruth were set down at the Merrills' door.

"We have had a beautiful time, Betty. We shall always remember *your* birthday," declared Ruth, and Winnie repeated the words.

Betty smiled and waved her hand; she realized that her two little friends were thanking her for more than their happy May-day.

Hero welcomed Ruth home, and seemed to be try-ing to tell her something. He ran around her, bark-ing and whining.

"What is it, Hero? What is the matter? Where is my mother?" she asked, as she pushed open the door of the sitting-room and found it vacant.

"Mother!" she called, running into the dining-room, and then heard her mother's voice calling from the kitchen:

"Come out here, Ruthie!"

Ruth stopped in the doorway with an exclamation of surprise.

"Oh, Mother! What is it?" she asked, for Mrs. Pennell was sitting in a low chair near the window, with one foot resting on a stool.

"I have sprained my ankle, Ruthie. I slipped com-ing in from the porch about an hour ago, and could just manage to crawl to this chair," replied Mrs. Pennell; "and now you will have to be 'mother' for a time. Tie my apron over your dress, and start up the fire, and fill the big kettle with water."

Ruth obeyed quickly, and in a few moments had carried out her mother's directions, bringing a small wooden tub in which to turn the water when it should be heated. She could think of nothing but that her mother must be in pain, as she drew off Mrs. Pennell is slipper and stocking, filled the tub, and now gently bathed the swollen ankle.

"Remember, Ruthie, dear, when any one has the ill-fortune to sprain wrist or ankle, that hot water is the best aid," Mrs. Pennell said, as she directed the way in which Ruth should bandage the ankle.

"I am afraid I am going to make a good deal of work for my little girl. We must try and send for your Aunt Clara to come as soon as possible," she added.

But Ruth did not mind the work; as she went from pantry to fireplace, preparing toast and a dish of hot gruel for her mother her thoughts flew away to Aunt Deborah at Barren Hill, to the lustre cup out of which Lafayette had drunk, and she realized that she could not go away from home now that her mother was lame.

After supper the ankle was bathed again, and now Mrs. Pennell thought it best that Ruth should run in and tell Mrs. Merrill of the accident, and ask her assistance. For she found herself unable to walk.

Mrs. Merrill came at once, and with her aid Mrs. Pennell was able to reach the big sofa in the sitting-room where she was made comfortable for the night.

"I will send Gilbert to Germantown early in the morning to fetch your sister," said Mrs. Merrill, as she bade her neighbor good-night.

"It is fortunate that Ruth had not started for her visit to Barren Hill," she added.

"It is, indeed. I could hardly spare her now," Mrs. Pennell responded.

Ruth listened with a feeling that there would never be any more happy days. Her mother was lame; she could not go to Barren Hill, and all her plans for visiting her father at Valley Forge, and perhaps seeing the brave young Lafayette, must be given up.

As she went slowly up-stairs to bed, she had almost forgotten the happy birthday picnic near the river. But she recalled what Black Jason had said of the rumor that General Howe was soon to leave Philadelphia. Just now, however, that seemed to be of little importance to Ruth. Her last waking thought was that she must be sure to get up early, very early, the next morning and have hot water ready to bathe the hurt ankle.

CHAPTER XVIII

A GREAT RESOLVE

ALTHOUGH Ruth was up in good season the next morning, she had only started the kitchen fire when Mrs. Merrill and Gilbert appeared at the kitchen door with a basket containing breakfast for Mrs. Pennell and Ruth.

Gilbert was all ready to start for his drive to Germantown, and, after a few words with Mrs. Pennell, hurried away.

Mrs. Merrill bathed the sprained ankle and helped Ruth's mother to a comfortable chair near the window.

"May I not put the little table by your chair, Mother, and have my breakfast here with you?" asked Ruth.

"Yes, indeed! That is exactly what I was wishing you to do, my dear," responded Mrs. Pennell; and Ruth ran away to the kitchen and brought in the hot corn bread that Mrs. Merrill had brought, the dish of porridge and the pot of steaming coffee. Then she drew a chair up opposite her mother, and they smiled happily at each other across the small table.

Mrs. Pennell declared that her foot was much better.

"I am sure your Aunt Clara will return with Gilbert," she continued, "but even then I am afraid you will have to do a good deal more than ever before, Ruthie, dear, for Aunt Clara is not yet fully recovered from her illness."

Ruth felt rather proud to know that her mother relied upon her to be of so much help, and, for the moment, quite forgot the visit to Barren Hill. She told her mother of all the delights of Betty's May-day party, and when she carried the breakfast dishes out to the kitchen she was almost her happy self again.

Winifred came over and helped Ruth with the household work that morning, and early in the afternoon Aunt Clara arrived; who, in spite of Mrs. Pennell's fears in regard to her strength, declared herself quite equal to taking care of her sister and attending to the work of the house.

Nevertheless Ruth was kept busy for a number of days; she did not go very far from her mother's sitting-room, and Mrs. Pennell said that her little daughter was "hands and feet" for her lame mother.

Mrs. Pennell's fingers were busy making a dress for Ruth. It was of white linen that Aunt Deborah had woven herself, and brought as a present to Ruth, and Mrs. Pennell was hemstitching the broad collar and dainty cuffs.

"Your Aunt Deborah will be pleased if you have the dress to wear when you visit her," said Mrs. Pennell, a few days after her accident, when Ruth sat beside her, both busy with their needles.

"But I can't go to Barren Hill, Mother. You couldn't spare me," replied Ruth.

"Of course you must go to Barren Hill. Not just at present; but in a week or two I shall be hobbling about the house, and your Aunt Clara will stay with me while you are away," said Mrs. Pennell.

"Truly? Am I really to go to Barren Hill?" exclaimed Ruth, dropping her work, and jumping up from her chair. "Oh! I'm so glad."

Mrs. Pennell looked at her little girl in surprise. She had had no idea how much Ruth had counted on this visit, nor with what disappointment she had given it up.

"Why, my dear child, you have not said a word about your visit since I hurt my ankle. I had not an idea that you wished to go so much," she said.

"I didn't wish to go when you couldn't take a step," Ruth declared.

"Well! I think it is almost worth while to have a sprained ankle to find out what a good little daughter I have," said her mother. "I feel very proud indeed. And now I think you had best put on your hat and go and make Betty Hastings an afternoon visit. It is nearly a week since her May party."

"I will ask Winifred to go, too," said Ruth eagerly, feeling happier than she had since her mother's accident.

"You had best change your dress, dear; put on your blue chambray," suggested her mother, and Ruth ran off to her own room, singing, "Joy is everywhere," as gaily as she had sung it when dancing around Betty's throne.

In a little while she was back in the sitting-room, all ready for her visit. In the pretty blue dress, and wearing a white hat with a blue ribbon around the crown, and with her white stockings and low shoes with shining silver buckles, Ruth was indeed a little girl of whom any mother might be proud.

Winifred was soon ready to accompany her, and the two friends started on their walk to see Betty Hastings.

As they came in sight of the Hastings house they both exclaimed in surprise. For on the steps was Betty, wearing her best hat, and the tall English officer, whose red coat Betty had borrowed for Gilbert's play, stood beside her.

"Do you suppose Betty is a prisoner?" whispered Winnie, a little fearfully.

"Of course she isn't, all dressed up in her best," replied Ruth, and at that moment Betty saw her two friends and waved her hand to them as she came down the steps beside the English officer.

"Oh, Winifred! Ruth! I am so glad you came. Now you can go with us to Walnut Grove and see the English officers practising for their tournament. Captain Harlow says you may go," she exclaimed, running forward to meet them.

Before Ruth or Winifred could reply the tall officer was beside Betty, and she now introduced him to her friends. Ruth and Winnie curtsied, with rather sober faces, and the Englishman bowed politely, and said that he should be happy to have Ruth and Winifred accompany them.

The young Englishman had lodged with Mrs. Hastings ever since the September day when the English army entered Philadelphia. He had been unfailingly kind to all the family, and when he offered to take Betty to Walnut Grove to see the preparations already well under way for the "Mischianza," as the soldiers named their famous entertainment to be given in honor of General Howe, Mrs. Hastings was quite willing for Betty to go.

"We shall be home in good season. I am sure your mothers would be willing," urged Betty, "and 'twill be a fine sight to-day, since the soldiers are to rehearse, as we did for Gilbert's play."

"Let's go, Ruth," Winifred whispered eagerly, and Ruth agreed, but with a vague feeling that she ought not to wish to be entertained by the amusements of America's enemies.

As they walked on toward Knight's Wharf, at the water edge of Green Street, where a boat was waiting to take Captain Harlow and his guests down the river to Mr. Wharton's country place, Ruth kept repeating the word "tournament" to herself, and wondering what it meant. Betty must know, she thought, for she had spoken it so easily. She resolved to ask her at the first opportunity.

A rowboat with two sailors was waiting for the captain, and he helped the little girls to the comfortable seats, and took his place at the tiller, and with a word to the oarsmen the boat moved out from the wharf and headed toward Southwark.

"What does 'tournament' mean, Betty?" Ruth whispered.

"Wait and see," laughed Betty.

"Does it mean the same as 'rehearsal'?" persisted Ruth.

"Not exactly," replied Betty, who only that very morning had asked her mother the same question. "It really means a make-believe battle," she explained, seeing Ruth's look of disappointment. "Men dress up in armor, such as soldiers used to wear, and their horses wear shields, and the men have long spears, and make-believe attack each other."

"Shall we see that to-day?" Ruth questioned.

But before Betty could answer she realized that Captain Harlow was speaking.

"I suppose you all know what the Knights of the days of Chivalry fought for?" he was saying, with a friendly smile at the three little American girls who were his guests.

"What are 'Knights'?" questioned Winifred.

"Can you answer that, Miss Betty?" asked the captain.

"Mother told me that a knight was a brave soldier, whose king gave him a sword, and then said: 'Arise, Sir Knight,'"replied Betty, while Ruth and Winifred listened admiringly, thinking their friend Betty must be the most clever girl in Philadelphia.

"Well, that is near enough," replied the young officer, "but I will tell you that in olden times knights used to have tilts, or tournaments, such as we mean to have on the eighteenth of this month. White Knights against the Knights of the Blended Rose."

It all sounded very wonderful to the three little girls, and Ruth was eager to reach Southwark, fearing that they might miss some part of this rehearsal.

The beautiful river was very still that pleasant afternoon in May, and the boat moved rapidly along, now and then passing some fishing-craft or pleasure boat, and the little girls smiled happily at each other, thinking that this indeed was a great adventure.

As the boat drew near the landing place, they could see a number of people on the wharf, and one of these Ruth at once recognized as Major André, the young officer who had introduced her to General Howe on the night when she had gone to demand the return of Hero.

Captain Harlow led the little girls to a bench on the further side of Mr. Wharton's beautiful lawn. "Stay here until I come after you," he said and hurried away.

The girls looked about admiringly. Just across the lawn from where they were sitting men were at work on a pavilion, in which the guests would be seated to view the "Mischianza." Soldiers on horseback were riding back and forth, and a trumpet call sent them all trotting away, to return immediately with long lances and shields on their left arms. Forming in two divisions they galloped forward and back, turning so quickly that Ruth and Betty both exclaimed, fearful that the riders would be thrown.

In a little while Captain Harlow came and took his guests to visit the ballroom. From the garden they ascended a short flight of steps, and entered a spacious hall, lined with mirrors. Never had the little girls seen anything so wonderful. Wherever they looked they saw Betty, Ruth, and Winifred all smiling with delight. Captain Harlow called a servant, and in a few moments the man returned with a silver tray on which were plates of candied fruits, cakes, and glasses of lemonade for his little guests.

"It's more wonderful than the May-day party," whispered Winifred.

But Ruth did not hear her. For at that moment two officers had entered the room.

"Sir Henry Clinton will arrive to-morrow, and General Howe will soon be on his way to England," she heard one of them say.

"'Tis a pity he cannot capture young Lafayette and take him back to England with him. King George would give him a royal welcome," responded the other.

"There is some such plan afoot," declared the first speaker.

"'Capture Lafayette!'" Ruth whispered the dreadful words over to herself and all her delight and pleasure vanished. These men, even the kind Captain Harlow, whom the Hastings liked so well, would try their best to capture the young French Republican, America's best friend, and take him to England a prisoner. Ruth could think of nothing else. She wondered if perhaps there was not already some plan by which Lafayette would be captured. She was very silent all the remainder of the afternoon, and Betty decided that Ruth must be tired.

But they all thanked the captain very politely for their pleasant visit, as he helped them from the boat and walked with them to Mrs. Hastings' door. Ruth was eager to get home. She meant to ask her mother if she might not go to Barren Hill very soon, perhaps to-morrow. It seemed to her she could hardly wait that long; for who could tell what the English soldiers might do before warning could reach Lafayette?

For Ruth had made a great resolve: she would try to let Lafayette know that the English General meant to do his best to take him a prisoner to England. Once at Barren Hill Ruth was sure that she could find some way to reach Washington's camp and warn the young Frenchman.

CHAPTER XIX

THE VISIT

RUTH'S mother and aunt listened to her account of her afternoon's adventure with interest, but when she had finished her mother said:

"I do not blame you, my dear, for accepting Betty's invitation, but I am surprised that Mrs. Hastings should permit an enemy of America's rights to become a friend, as it is evident she so regards the young English officer who lodges there."

In her heart Ruth agreed with her mother. It seemed disloyal even to have accepted Betty's invitation. Nevertheless Ruth was glad that she had gone to Southwark; for the conversation she had overheard in regard to Lafayette seemed of great importance to the little girl. She did not speak to any one of what she had heard the English officers say, but she could not explain even to herself why she had not at once told Winnie, or why she did not now tell her mother. It seemed to Ruth that it was a secret which she could confide only to one person: to Lafayette himself.

"May I go to Barren Hill to-morrow, Mother, dear?" she asked earnestly, as she bade her mother good-night.

"Why, Ruthie! Of course not! Your things are not ready, and we have not sent Aunt Deborah word to have Farmer Withely call for you," replied her mother in surprise. "Why are you so anxious to go to-morrow?"

"Oh, Mother! Never mind about my things. And I am sure Farmer Withely will take me," urged Ruth.

"But do you think it will be quite fair to Aunt Clara?" said Mrs. Pennell gravely. "You know there are many things you can do to help her until I am on my feet again. Be patient, Ruthie. You shall go to Barren Hill as soon as it is possible."

Ruth was ready to cry with disappointment as she went up-stairs to bed. For a moment she had been tempted to tell her mother her reason for wanting to go at once to Barren Hill, but she realized that her mother might say that a little girl could do nothing to protect a great soldier, and forbid her making any attempt to reach the young Frenchman only to repeat the careless talk of English soldiers.

"I must do it myself, in some way. I must!" thought Ruth as she prepared for bed. She wondered if Aunt Clara would not help her in her plan to go to Barren Hill.

Ruth was late to breakfast the next morning, and Aunt Clara wondered a little at her sober face, while Mrs. Pennell was troubled, thinking that Ruth was brooding over her disappointment in not going to Barren Hill.

The little girl performed her usual household duties; but when her mother suggested that she should go and play with Winifred, she shook her head.

In the afternoon she went into the yard with Hero and "Cecilia" to the seat under the maple tree. Aunt Clara noticed that the little girl sat looking across the garden as if her thoughts were far away, neglecting Cecilia, and paying no attention to the faithful Hero.

"I am afraid Ruthie is going to be ill," she said to Mrs. Pennell. "She has not seemed like herself since she got home from her visit yesterday."

Mrs. Pennell was quite sure that Ruth was not ill, but she was troubled that her little daughter should be so disappointed and unwilling to postpone the visit to Aunt Deborah.

"Her heart is set on going to Barren Hill, and I have told her she must wait a while," she explained.

"But why not let her go now?" suggested Aunt Clara. "She is a good and helpful child, and deserves the pleasure. I can make her things ready."

It did not take much persuasion for Mrs. Pennell to give her consent, and when Ruth came slowly into the sitting-room, in response to Aunt Clara's call, her mother said:

"Well, my dear, your Aunt Clara says that you well deserve to start for Barren Hill as soon as she can make you ready. So be on the outlook for Farmer

Withely to-morrow morning, and ask him to call for you on Thursday, and to tell Aunt Deborah to expect you."

Ruth's face had brightened as her mother began to speak, but as Mrs. Pennell finished she was again almost ready to cry.

" 'Thursday'!" she repeated. "That's two whole days to wait! Why can't I go to-morrow?" she said anxiously.

Mrs. Pennell looked at Ruth in surprise. Never before had she known her little daughter to whine, or seem to want her own way more than anything else.

"What is the matter, Ruth? I thought you would be so glad that your Aunt Clara had persuaded me to let you go so soon. If you say anything about going before Thursday we shall give up the visit altogether," she said.

Ruth hardly knew what to say or do. It seemed to the little girl that her delay in starting for Barren Hill meant the possibility of the capture of Lafayette. She was tempted to tell her mother the reason for wishing to start at once, but she was sure Mrs. Pennell would promptly forbid her carrying out her plan to visit Valley Forge.

Ruth managed to thank her mother for permission to go on Thursday, and to say that she would be sure and see Farmer Withely and give him the message the next morning, and then went back to her seat in the garden. She had just taken up Cecilia, when the garden gate was pushed open and Winifred came running up the path.

"Gilbert says he is ashamed of me!" declared Winifred, "and of you, and of Betty Hastings, for going to Southwark yesterday," and she looked at Ruth a little fearfully, as if expecting her friend to be quite overcome by Gilbert's disapproval.

"I don't care if he is," was Ruth's surprising reply. "I am glad I went, and I always shall be glad. And perhaps some day Gilbert will be glad too."

"Why, Ruth Pennell!" exclaimed Winifred.

"You tell him just what I say," insisted Ruth, beginning to feel more cheerful at the thought of Gilbert's surprise when he should discover that she had saved Lafayette from capture through her visit to Southwark. After all, Thursday was only the day after to-morrow, she reflected, and the English were too much occupied in their welcome to Sir Henry Clinton to start off to capture the young Frenchman. Besides that encouraging thought Winifred had brought over a box filled with beads. They were wonderful beads—blue, all shades of blue, and sparkling red beads, and beads of shining green, and white beads as clear as dew-drops.

"You may pick out those you like best," said she generous Winnie, "enough to make you a necklace, and one for Cecilia, too," and the two little girls were soon happily occupied with the beads, and Ruth forgot all about her fears lest her warning should come too late. But when Winifred jumped up saying that it was time for her to go home, Ruth remembered that she had not told Winnie that she was to go to Barren Hill on Thursday.

"Oh, Ruth! Then you won't see all the processions for Captain Harlow's entertainment. And he said this morning when I went over to see Betty that we could go down again, the very day before it is given," exclaimed Winifred.

"I wouldn't go if I were at home," declared Ruth, "but don't you tell Gilbert that I said I wouldn't go. You tell him what I said first: 'that I am glad I went, and I always shall be glad. And that perhaps some day he will be glad too that I went to Southwark.'"

Winifred promised to deliver the message. She did not suppose it had any special meaning, but she was sure it would puzzle Gilbert.

The next day was a busy one for Ruth. Farmer Withely promised to call for her on Thursday afternoon, and wondered to himself why the little girl was so eager to visit Barren Hill. Mrs. Pennell finished the white linen dress, while Ruth helped Aunt Clara in the work of the house, packed the small leathern trunk, which was to accompany her on her journey, and last of all dressed Cecilia in her best,

THE BIG HORSE TROTTED DOWN THE STREET

for she had decided, at Aunt Clara's suggestion, that Cecilia needed a visit to the country.

Mrs. Pennell could now walk a little, and not until Thursday morning did Ruth have a single doubt in regard to going away from home. But as the time of her departure drew near she kept close beside her mother, and when Aunt Clara called that Farmer Withely was driving down the street Ruth was suddenly quite sure that she could not go and leave her mother behind.

"Oh, Mother! I don't wish to go," she exclaimed, her arms close about her mother's neck.

Mrs. Pennell held her close, telling her of the beautiful time she would have with Aunt Deborah. "And, who knows! You may see Lafayette himself," she added, knowing how great a hero the young Frenchman seemed to all American children, as well as to their elders. "I shall come home soon," Ruth answered earnestly, and then Aunt Clara called that Farmer Withely was waiting, and with one more good-bye kiss Ruth ran down the steps, and in a few moments was seated beside the farmer, while the big horse trotted down the street

Aunt Clara had put a box on the wagon seat beside Ruth. "Open it when you are half-way to your journey's end," she had said smilingly, and Farmer Withely had smiled also, and nodded approvingly, thinking to himself that he had no better customers than the Pennell family, and being quite sure of the appetizing contents of the box.

As they drove out of the town, past the stone house, and on to the river road Ruth pointed out the field, where the May-pole was still standing, and told the farmer all the May-day sports and songs.

"Perhaps you could remember some of those songs, Miss Ruth? Now, if you could, I should admire to hear them," said Farmer Withely.

"Yes, indeed! I remember every one," said Ruth, and when she began Mrs. Hastings' song, Farmer Withely found that it was one he too used to sing as a boy on far-off May-days, and so they sang it together, their voices falling pleasantly on the sweet spring air.

Then Ruth ventured to ask if Farmer Withely had ever seen General Washington, or, perhaps, young Lafayette?

"Indeed I have. My best gray horse has now the honor of belonging to General Washington, and many a cold journey have I taken to carry food to the soldiers at Valley Forge," responded Farmer Withely, and he went on to tell of the unfaltering courage of the American soldiers through the hardships at the camp.

He told of young Lafayette's recent return to Valley Forge from Albany, and of his devotion to the American cause. Ruth listened eagerly to all he had to tell her, and the miles slipped away behind them, and when Farmer Withely pointed toward the old church, which stood near the summit of Barren Hill, and said that they had nearly reached their journey's end, Ruth declared that it had been a very pleasant journey, and Farmer Withely said he would like just such a passenger every day.

Aunt Deborah Farleigh was at the gate to welcome her little niece, and then Ruth had to be taken and introduced to the bees, and to see two brown calves in the barnyard, and a flock of fine chickens.

After that it was nearly dusk and supper was ready, and it was not until Ruth took her seat at the table that she remembered her real errand to Barren Hill.

"Aunt Deborah, the English have not captured Lafayette, have they?" she asked earnestly.

For once Aunt Deborah was startled from her usual calmness.

"For pity's sake, child! What dost thou mean?" she responded. "I have heard naught of such a thing."

Ruth gave a sigh of relief. "I just wanted to be sure," she replied.

CHAPTER XX

THE May sun streamed warmly into the big square chamber where Ruth slept, and she awoke to the song of birds, and the fragrance of blossoming lilacs.

For a few moments she lay quite still, looking wonderingly about the room. It seemed a "shining" room to Ruth, with its whitewashed walls, and its smooth polished floor, and only a chest of drawers, a light-stand and a rush-bottomed chair for furniture.

She got up and dressed slowly, wondering if her mother missed her very much, and if Hero would go scratching and whining to her door in search of his little mistress. Aunt Deborah's house was much larger than the little brick house which was Ruth's home in Philadelphia, and, as Ruth came slowly down the wide stairs she thought what a fine house it would be for little girls to live in; there seemed so much room and so little furniture.

Aunt Deborah lived alone, but the Withely farm adjoined hers, and Farmer Withely took care of her farm and stock.

"Good-morning, Ruth," said Aunt Deborah with her sunny smile, as her little niece came into the big kitchen to find breakfast awaiting her. "I trust thy pleasure in being here is as great as mine in having thee. And I have great news for thee. Thy dear father came over from Valley Forge a week ago, and was sorry enough to find thee not here. And he had great tidings for me. He says that France has now joined with America in the war against England, and Washington hopes for great aid from so powerful an ally."

"Oh, Aunt Deborah! Won't my father come again?" responded Ruth. "May I not go to Valley Forge to see him?"

"It may be that he will come again," Aunt Deborah replied thoughtfully. "And who knows but he may come with Lafayette! For General Washington is sending scouting parties about the country to discover the plans of the English. So any day we may see the troops of either army come marching up the road."

Ruth was almost too excited to eat her breakfast after listening to Aunt Deborah's news, and even the sight of the pink lustre cup from which Lafayette had drunk seemed of little consequence. If English soldiers came marching that way Ruth knew well that their purpose would be to capture American scouting parties, and she became more eager than ever to go to Valley Forge, and again asked Aunt Deborah if she could not go. But Aunt

Deborah promptly responded that such a visit was impossible.

"'Tis a ride of over ten miles, and a ford to cross, she said. "Farmer Withely has no spare time at present to take thee; besides that, General Washington does not care for visitors."

Ruth looked so disappointed that Aunt Deborah added: "And who knows what day Lafayette may ride this way again? It may even be this very morning! Take thy doll and walk to the church; from there thou canst see both ways. If the English redcoats come along the river road thee must hasten back and tell me, so that we may start some one off at once to warn our American soldiers."

"Might I go?" asked Ruth.

"How could a small girl like thee cross the Schuylkill?" questioned Aunt Deborah. "'Tis most likely I should have to go myself."

Ruth now felt that she could really be of use if she kept watch from the top of Barren Hill, and she ran through the garden, and climbed up the rough slope to the little square church, from whose steps she could watch the quiet road which curved along by the woods to the riverside. She thought of Hero, and wished it had been possible to bring him with her. "Just for company," she whispered to herself, for she began to feel that she was a long way from home.

"Unless Father or Lafayette comes to-day I must go to Valley Forge to-morrow," she resolved.

But the day passed without a sign of any advancing troops, and at supper-time Ruth was so quiet and sober that Aunt Deborah began to fear that her little niece was homesick, and tried to amuse her by telling her of a tame squirrel who lived in the woodshed and had made friends with a family of kittens. But the little girl did not seem interested; she wanted to know if the water was very deep at Matson's ford, and how long it would take to walk to Valley Forge; until Aunt Deborah wondered if Ruth really thought such a journey possible for a little girl. She recalled the visit Ruth had made to the English General in order to rescue Hero, and said to herself that she was sure Ruth would not again undertake any plan without asking permission.

"I'll wait until to-morrow," Ruth resolved, as she went to bed that night. "I mustn't wait any longer," and comforted by that resolution she was soon fast asleep.

She awoke before daylight, to find Aunt Deborah standing beside the bed.

"Get up, my dear child. Lose no time. General Lafayette is below, and I am preparing his breakfast," she said.

"Oh, Aunt Deborah!" exclaimed Ruth, sure that this was a dream from which she would soon awake.

"Hasten, child, if thou wouldst see him," and Aunt Deborah, candle in hand, disappeared from the shadowy room.

Ruth dressed more quickly than ever before, but she did not neglect to brush her hair neatly, but not until she opened the kitchen door did she realize that the strings to her stout leather shoes were unfastened.

It was broad daylight now, and the morning sunshine was all about the Marquis de Lafayette as he looked up with a smiling nod to the little girl who stood gazing at him from the doorway.

"If thee please, sir, this is my niece, Ruth Pennell, who has long cherished the hope of seeing thee," said Aunt Deborah.

The young Frenchman rose from his seat, and bowed as ceremoniously as if Lady Washington herself stood before him.

Ruth could think only of her thick shoes and the wandering strings, as she endeavored to make a proper curtsy.

Lafayette was in the uniform of an American officer, and two American soldiers were on guard at the open door. The little party had ridden over from Valley Forge under cover of the night to discover a camping-ground for a body of troops which Lafayette was soon to lead toward Philadelphia, for

Washington had discovered that Sir Henry Clinton had orders to evacuate the city.

"Will you not share my breakfast, Mistress Ruth?" asked the young Frenchman, drawing one of the high-backed wooden chairs to the table beside his own.

"The child will indeed be honored," replied Aunt Deborah, and almost before Ruth could realize the great honor in store for her she found herself seated at the table. She looked up to find Lafayette smiling at her shy word of thanks.

What a wonderful breakfast for any little girl to have to remember. Ruth wished with all her heart that Winifred and Gilbert could see her.

"I have a small daughter of my own in France," said the kind young Frenchman, "and I hear that your father is at Valley Forge."

"Yes, sir," responded Ruth faintly, wondering to herself why she did not at once tell him what she had heard the English officers at Southwark say of General Howe's intention to capture him.

"Well, very soon he will be safe at home," continued Lafayette. And now Ruth resolved to speak.

"If you please, sir —" she began, but at that moment Lafayette sprang to his feet, and with a word of thanks to Aunt Deborah for her hospitality, and a smiling nod to Ruth, he started toward the door, saying:

"I have indeed lingered too long. I must lose no time in getting back to camp."

But now Ruth was out of her chair in a second; she was no longer in awe of the young Frenchman.

"I must tell you. I heard two Englishmen say you were to be captured and taken to England," she declared eagerly, running along by his side.

The young man smiled down at the eager, half frightened child.

"Ah, well, *ma chère*, they have been saying that for a long time," he responded lightly, "but thou art a kind little maid to warn me; and I assure thee I will remember it," and with a word of farewell he hurried across the garden, mounted his horse, and in a few moments had vanished behind the thick growing trees.

Aunt Deborah and Ruth stood on the garden path listening until they could no longer hear the sound of the horses' feet on the hard country road. Then Aunt Deborah smiled at Ruth.

"Thee should be a happy girl now, I am sure," she said, "and thee did right to tell him what his enemies threaten. Perhaps that was one reason thee was so anxious to visit Valley Forge?"

"Oh, yes, Aunt Deborah! If he had not come I should have had to run away so he might surely be warned," Ruth responded.

"I would have taken the message myself had need been," said Aunt Deborah; "but thee sees that he already knew of their wicked plan. He did but smile at such a threat."

A few days after this visit there was great excitement on Barren Hill. A troop of American soldiers, the very flower of Washington's army, commanded by Lafayette, were in camp on the hill. Farmers were bringing buckets of milk and freshly baked bread for the soldiers' breakfast, and Ruth could see and hear the bustle of the camps.

At first Mistress Farleigh and Ruth had hoped that Ruth's father might be one of the company, but as the day passed and he did not appear at the stone house they became sure that he was still at Valley Forge.

Mistress Farleigh had told Ruth not to go to the summit of the hill where the troops were camped.

"Thee may walk toward the river, or in the paths at the edge of the wood," Aunt Deborah had said, adding that she wished Hero were at Barren Hill. "Then thee could go wherever thee pleased."

But that day Ruth was content to play with Cecilia in the pleasant garden, hoping until long after sunset that her father might appear.

Neither Aunt Deborah nor Ruth slept well that night, and both were up very early in the morning. After their simple breakfast Aunt Deborah busied herself with bread making, that she might send hot corn bread to the American soldiers.

"And wilt thou not run over to Farmer Withely's and ask Mistress Withely for the loan of a covered basket of good size, Ruth," she suggested, and Ruth willingly obeyed. The Withely farmhouse was at the further side of a broad field, and hidden by a small grove of pine trees. It was a pleasant walk in the early morning, and as Ruth ran along she could see that the American troops were harnessing their horses, and that it was evident some movement was at hand.

"Oh! Perhaps I shall never see Lafayette again, and I did not help him after all," she thought.

And now another and more startling sound came to Ruth's ears. Along the Ridge road she could hear the sound of horses' feet and the rattle of musketry.

"Perhaps it is more American soldiers coming," thought the little girl. But she felt vaguely troubled, as she went slowly on. She had just entered the little woodland path which led to Farmer Withely's when she saw a glimmer of a red coat in the underbrush.

Ruth stopped, and crouched low behind a small tree. She heard low voices, and in a moment a laughing voice said:

"We have the fine Frenchman just where we want him. He is preparing his men to receive Howe's soldiers on the Ridge road, but he does not dream that General Grant with seven thousand troops is coming up in his rear. General Howe has invited a dinner party to meet Lafayette to-night in Philadelphia."

"'Tis a fine thing to get the Frenchman," came the low response; "we'd better move farther up the hill now."

For a moment Ruth hesitated, hardly realizing the importance of what she had overheard. Then she turned and ran toward the American encampment, where she could see troops of soldiers already moving forward toward the Ridge road.

"Oh! suppose I do not get there in time to tell him that there is an English army coming behind him," she thought.

Once she stumbled and fell over an unseen root; but at last breathless and tired she found herself facing a number of American soldiers, one of whom called out:

"Run home, child; you are in danger here."

"Lafayette! Lafayette!" she called wildly. "Tell him there are thousands of English soldiers coming up the road behind his army. The road from Swedes Ford," called Ruth.

Almost before Ruth finished speaking one of the soldiers had turned his horse and galloped away to find his commander, and tell him of this unexpected enemy. Ruth turned and hurried home. She had entirely forgotten about her errand to Farmer Withely's.

CHAPTER XXI

AT HOME

LAFAYETTE had received the startling news and acted upon it without a question. He marched his men rapidly toward Matson's Ford, on the lower road, and when the British generals came up to Barren Hill they were astonished to find that they had only each other to fight. They decided not to cross the river, but returned to Philadelphia, much disappointed that the Marquis de Lafayette was not their prisoner.

Lafayette likewise marched back to Valley Forge, where he was received with great joy.

The soldier who had taken Ruth's message found an opportunity to tell Lafayette that the news that had saved his army had been brought by a little girl.

"She came running up the hill calling your name, sir. A little girl with yellow hair and blue eyes," said the soldier.

"Would you know her if you saw her again?" questioned the young Frenchman.

"I should indeed, sir," was the quick reply.

Aunt Deborah had not questioned Ruth when, flushed and tired, she came running back to the

179

house on the morning when the Americans had so easily made their escape, thanks to Ruth's message, from the overwhelming armies of the English. For a number of days Ruth did not venture beyond the garden, and when, a week later, her father opened the gate and called "Ruth!" she ran to meet him, feeling sure that now everything was sure to come right, and that she and her father could soon return to Philadelphia.

But Mr. Pennell was not alone; there was a tall smiling soldier just behind him, and near the gate a graceful figure on horseback that Ruth recognized as Lafayette.

Aunt Deborah came hurrying to welcome Mr. Pennell; the soldier had turned back, and was standing beside the mounted officer, who soon dismounted and came slowly up the path.

"Lieutenant Pennell, I have to thank your little maid for a very great service," he said, as he took Ruth's hand, and smiled down on the little girl; and then he told first of Ruth's warning that his capture was planned by General Howe, and then of her warning of an advancing army against his troops.

"I came this morning that I might thank her for her loyal service to America and to me," he said, bending low to kiss the warm little hand that rested in his own.

It was indeed a wonderful day for Ruth Pennell.

After Lafayette rode away she told the story to her surprised and astonished father, while Aunt Deborah listened as if she could hardly believe her own ears.

Lieutenant Pennell had been given a week's furlough, and was quite sure that it would be possible for him to visit his home in Philadelphia, taking Ruth with him, for the English were leaving the city as rapidly as possible.

Later in the day Aunt Deborah told Ruth's father of his little daughter's visit to General Howe, and Ruth told of Gilbert's play, and of the boy's arrest by the English, of Betty's capture on account of the borrowed coat, and of her escape from the house by the river.

"The children of Philadelphia will indeed remember the year of 1778, and surely my little daughter can never forget it," responded her father.

Ruth was eager to start for home as soon as possible, especially as Aunt Deborah said that she must return in midsummer with her mother for a longer visit. "And thy friend Winifred must come also," she had added.

Winifred and Gilbert had heard the story of Ruth's warning to the American army, for Aunt Deborah had sent a letter to Mrs. Pennell at the first opportunity, and Gilbert had at once declared that he would "make up a play" about it.

"And we will have it the very day Ruth comes home," he said. "I will be Lafayette, and Ruth can be herself."

"And let's ask Betty and all the girls who went to the May party," suggested Winifred.

"And Ned, too, and Mother and Mrs. Pennell," agreed Gilbert. "I tell you, it is lucky Ruth went to Barren Hill, and I guess it's lucky you girls went to Southwark that day. You see, it put Ruth on the lookout to warn Lafayette," he added.

Gilbert's second play proved even a greater success than his first. The girls listened admiringly to Winifred's account of Lafayette's thanking Ruth, and when the guests had all gone the two little friends went to their favorite seat in Ruth's garden under the big maple tree. Hero kept very close to his little mistress, as if afraid that she might again suddenly disappear.

"Do you remember that day when we began the chair for Cecilia, Ruthie?" asked Winifred, "and when you said you wished you could do some great service for Lafayette because he had come to help America?"

Ruth nodded, not quite sure of the exact day, but very sure that she had always wanted to help the young Frenchman, and wondering what Winifred would say next.

"And now you have done him a great service," Winifred continued soberly. "And Betty and Annette, and all the girls say that you are a real heroine."

"I guess they don't know much about heroines," responded Ruth, but there was a pleased smile about her mouth. Of course any little girl whose hand had been kissed by Lafayette was a heroine, she thought happily.